Battle Orders • 18

British Commandos 1940–46

Tim Moreman

Consultant Editor Dr Duncan Anderson • *Series editors* Marcus Cowper and Nikolai Bogdanovic

First published in Great Britain in 2006 by Osprey Publishing,
Midland House, West Way, Botley, Oxford OX2 0PH, United Kingdom.
443 Park Avenue South, New York, NY 10016, USA
Email: info@ospreypublishing.com

ISBN 978 1 84176 986 8

Editorial by Ilios Publishing, Oxford, UK (www.iliospublishing.com)
Design: Bounford.com
Index by Alan Thatcher
Originated by The Electronic Page Company, Cwmbran, UK
Typeset in Monotype Gill Sans and ITC Stone Serif
08 09 10 11 12 11 10 9 8 7 6 5 4 3 2

A CIP catalogue record for this book is available from the British Library.

For a catalogue of all books published by Osprey Military and Aviation please contact:
Osprey Direct, C/o Random House Distribution Center, 400 Hahn Road,
Westminster, MD 21157
Email: info@ospreydirect.com

Osprey Direct UK, P.O. Box 140, Wellingborough, Northants, NN8 2FA, UK
E-mail: info@ospreydirect.co.uk

www.ospreypublishing.com

Image credits

The photos in this book come from the Imperial War Museum's huge collections, which cover all aspects of conflict involving Britain and the Commonwealth since the start of the 20th century. These rich resources are available online to search, browse and buy at www.iwmcollections.org.uk. In addition to Collections Online, you can visit the Visitor Rooms where you can explore over 8 million photographs, thousands of hours of moving images, the largest sound archive of its kind in the world, thousands of diaries and letters written by people in wartime, and a huge reference library. To make an appointment, call (020) 7416 5320, or e-mail mail@iwm.org.uk.

Author's note

In the tree diagrams and maps in this volume, the units and movements of national forces are depicted in the following colours:

British/Canadian	Brown
Japanese	Red
German	Grey

For a key to the symbols used in this volume, see below.

Measurements

Distances, ranges, and dimensions are mostly given in inches, feet, yards, and statute miles. A simple conversion table is provided below.

feet to metres:	multiply feet by 0.3048
yards to metres	multiply yards by 0.9114
miles to kilometres	multiply miles by 1.6093
centimetres to inches	multiply centimetres by 0.3937

Key to military symbols

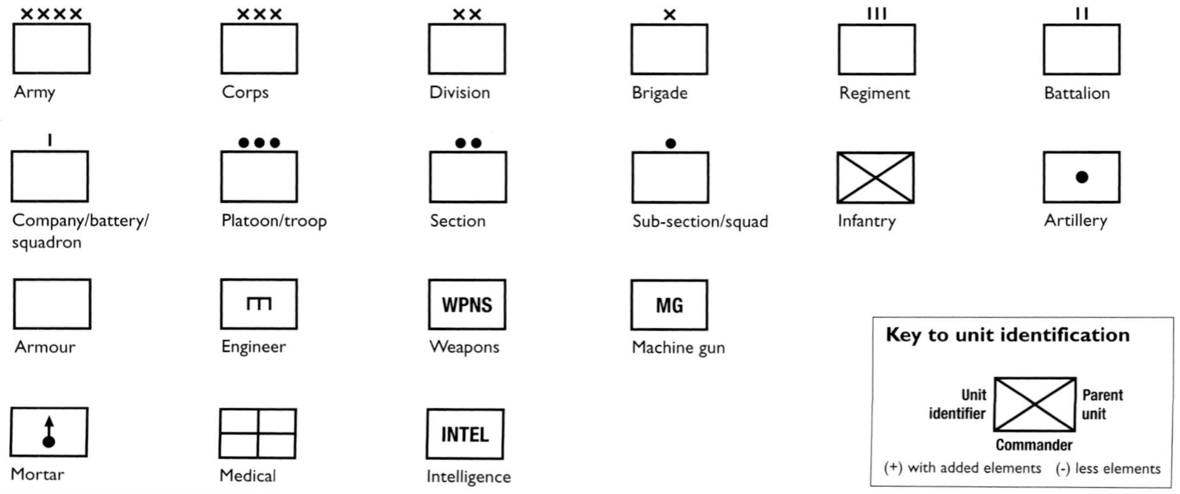
XXXX
Army
XXX
Corps
XX
Division
X
Brigade
III
Regiment
II
Battalion
I
Company/battery/ squadron
Platoon/troop
Section
Sub-section/squad
Infantry
Artillery
Armour
Engineer
WPNS
Weapons
MG
Machine gun
Mortar
Medical
INTEL
Intelligence
Key to unit identification
Unit identifier
Parent unit
Commander
(+) with added elements
(-) less elements

Contents

Introduction 4

Combat mission 6

Organization 9

Formation and early organization • The formation of the Special Service Brigade
The 1941 reorganization and the expansion of the SSB • The Commandos in the Middle East
The growth of the SSB: Royal Marine, Inter-Allied, and other new Commandos
The April 1943 expansion of and changes to the SSB

Doctrine and training 33

Achnacarry – the Commando Depot • Training from late 1943 to the end of the war

Tactics 42

Commando uniform, equipment and weapons 45

Command, control, communications and intelligence 48

Combat operations 53

Operation *Ambassador*: Guernsey, July 1940 • Operation *Claymore*: the 1941 raid on the Lofoten Islands
Operations *Anklet* and *Archery*: the 1941 raid on Vaagso • 'The greatest raid of all': Operation
Chariot – No. 2 Commando at St Nazaire, 1942 • Operation *Infatuate*: the 1944 assault on Walcheren
The battle for Hill 170: 3rd Commando Brigade in Arakan, February 1945

Lessons learned 83

Chronology 86

Select bibliography 88

Abbreviations 89

Endnotes 90

Appendices 91

Appendix 1: outline history of Commando units, 1940–45 • Appendix 2: Commando battle honours

Index 95

Introduction

This book looks at the British Commandos (both Army and later Royal Marine) initially raised in the United Kingdom in June 1940, within days of the ignominious evacuation of Dunkirk, to strike back hard and effectively against German-occupied Europe. Formed at Prime Minister Winston Churchill's direct request, these elite troops, all picked volunteers drawn from the ranks of regular British Army units and newly formed Independent Companies, employed highly aggressive irregular fighting methods while carrying out their specialist role of mounting 'butcher and bolt' or 'hit and run' raids from the sea. No organization of this unique type had existed before as part of the Order of Battle of the British Army or Royal Marines, although numerous such raids had been conducted during the long history of the British armed forces. New fighting and training methods had to be quickly developed to take the war to the German Wehrmacht. The first sea-borne raids, mounted within days of the Commandos formation, were often shambles and amounted to little more than pin pricks against the Wehrmacht, during which the learning curve for both officers and men of these new units, part of a new Special Service Brigade, proved extremely steep. Similar problems were encountered by other Commando units organized, equipped and trained during 1940 to hit back against the Germans and Italians in the Middle East.

The Axis powers were not the only opponents encountered by the Commandos, however, during the early war years. Not everyone in the UK welcomed this new organization. Indeed, the Commandos met strong opposition and intense dislike, and aroused deep suspicion within the senior ranks of the British Army, many of whom accused them of diverting resources away from the 'real war' and stripping regular units of their best officers and men. As Mike Chappell has written: 'The history of the Commandos is a tale of triumph and disaster, of bureaucratic wrangling over their employment, and of hostility endured at the hands of the military establishment.'[1]

The Commandos soon proved their distinct worth, however, as part of the quickly expanding wartime British Army. A series of successful sea-borne attacks growing in size and complexity during 1940–42, including the Lofoten Islands, Vaagso, and St Nazaire against *Festung Europa*, meant the Commandos were quickly lionized by the British public (starved of successes during the early war as they stood alone in defiance of Nazi Germany) and also quickly inspired fear amongst their opponents. An enduring image of the Commandos as bold, daring and reckless raiders taking the war directly to the Germans soon took root, a result of widespread publicity and skilful propaganda, which endures to this day. As esprit de corps and skill increased and appropriate organization, equipment, and training was developed for their highly specialized role, the Commandos achieved results far out of proportion to their small size during a succession of hit-and-run raids growing in size and daring from the sea into North-West Europe, Scandinavia, Italy and the Middle East. The high morale, esprit de corps, and combat effectiveness achieved by the Commandos was second to none in the British Army. Indeed, the glowing results achieved meant the order of battle of the Special Service Brigade was steadily augmented as World War II progressed, with the addition of various specialized units and eventually nine Royal Marine Commandos. Even so, the number of men actually employed, relative to the rest of the British armed forces, remained small. For the next four years the Commandos were constantly in action, from the snows of Norway to the jungles of South East Asia, from islands in the

Men of No. 4 Commando being briefed before D-Day, June 1944. (B5098)

Adriatic to the beaches of Normandy. By the end of the war their role, moreover, had changed, with Commandos increasingly taking their place in the fighting alongside regular units, although they still retained their elite status. Indeed, by the end of the war the Commandos increasingly were deployed in larger formations, with four Special Service Brigades employed to spearhead major amphibious landings and seize particularly difficult objectives in advance of conventional troops, as demonstrated during the Normandy landings, the Walcheren operations, and during the Third Arakan campaign in Burma. A range of other highly specialized Special Forces, moreover, were directly inspired by the Commandos' example, including the Special Air Service, Special Boat Service and the Parachute Regiment, as well as other Commando units in other Commonwealth armies. The Australian Army, for example, formed a range of Independent Companies/Commandos, that served widely in the Far East. A direct lineage can also be traced from the Commandos to the US Army's elite Rangers formed in June 1942, whose 1st Ranger Battalion underwent instruction at a Commando training establishment and who received their baptism of fire while understudying No. 3 and No. 4 Commandos during the 1942 Dieppe raid.

This book charts the changing order of battle of the elite British Commandos during World War II. It looks in turn at their combat mission, tactics, doctrine and training and evolving organization. It also looks at five carefully selected combat operations: the first raid involving the Commandos on the island of Guernsey; the Lofoten Islands raid; the Vaagso raid; the attack on St Nazaire; the Walcheren landings; and the role of No. 3 Commando Brigade in Arakan during the closing stages of the war in the Far East. It concludes by highlighting the lasting lessons learned from their employment during World War II. However, it should be noted from the outset that this book does not look at the various small, highly specialized units that formed part of the Special Service Brigade, or that bore the Commando title during the course of the conflict, due to space restrictions; instead, the focus is deliberately on the main combat units. Unfortunately, the work of the Royal Navy Beachhead Commandos, for example (who oversaw beachheads secured after amphibious landings), and the Royal Air Force's Servicing Commandos (whose task was to secure and manage newly captured airfields), lie outside the scope of this study, although both underwent specialized Commando training. Similarly the smaller, highly specialized units raised under the auspices of Combined Operations organization – such as the Combined Operations Assault Pilotage Parties and Royal Marine Boom Patrol Unit – must await a further study.

Combat mission

The newly raised Commandos were assigned a combat mission in June 1940 very different from that of the rest of the British Army, itself primarily occupied with re-organizing, re-training and re-equipping for the defence of the UK against an imminent German invasion. It involved mounting a series of small-scale, hit-and-run, amphibious raids and harassing operations along the lengthy shoreline of Nazi-occupied Europe and Norway. By doing so the Commandos would take the war to the enemy and strike back hard and hopefully effectively against the might of the Wehrmacht, thereby boosting flagging military and public morale, tying down enemy troops, and keeping them permanently on their toes.

The scale of individual Commando operations and the organization chosen for them varied considerably depending on the situation, fully exploiting their flexibility and the individual resourcefulness and skill of their men. Attacks varied from minor raids involving a handful of picked men, a single Fighting Troop, an individual Commando, building up to a major landing involving several complete Commando units working in cooperation with attached regular troops. Inter-service support and close cooperation was always vital to land and support raiding forces. A wide range of objectives was chosen to fulfill their combat mission, including the destruction of key enemy facilities (such as coastal fortresses and batteries, radar stations, and other fixed defences), killing enemy troops, diverting attention away from other combat operations, and spreading 'alarm and despondency' amongst the occupying forces. Fixing

Lord Lovat and Lt Col Robert Laycock at Newhaven following the Dieppe raid. (H22582)

the attention of the enemy and tying down large numbers of troops in static guard duties was an indirect objective of growing importance. Another critical part of the combat mission assigned to the Commandos, either during the course of other raids or during specific operations, was intelligence gathering. This important task included the capture of German prisoners, the collection of technical manuals and documents, and the seizure of examples of enemy arms and equipment. Much the same skills were required by troops involved in either type of operation, but those gathering intelligence normally deliberately eschewed contact with the enemy to achieve their objective. Initially, beach and ground reconnaissance was also part of the task given to these elite troops, with information desperately needed about enemy defences,

The Combined Operations badge
A distinctive Combined Operations sleeve badge or patch was designed early in 1942, and with Lord Louis Mountbatten's express approval was issued towards the end of the year. It was normally worn married up with a uniform Command shoulder title, which had the number of each unit followed by the word 'Commando' in red lettering on a dark blue background. Early in 1945 it was replaced by a new Commando Group sleeve badge.

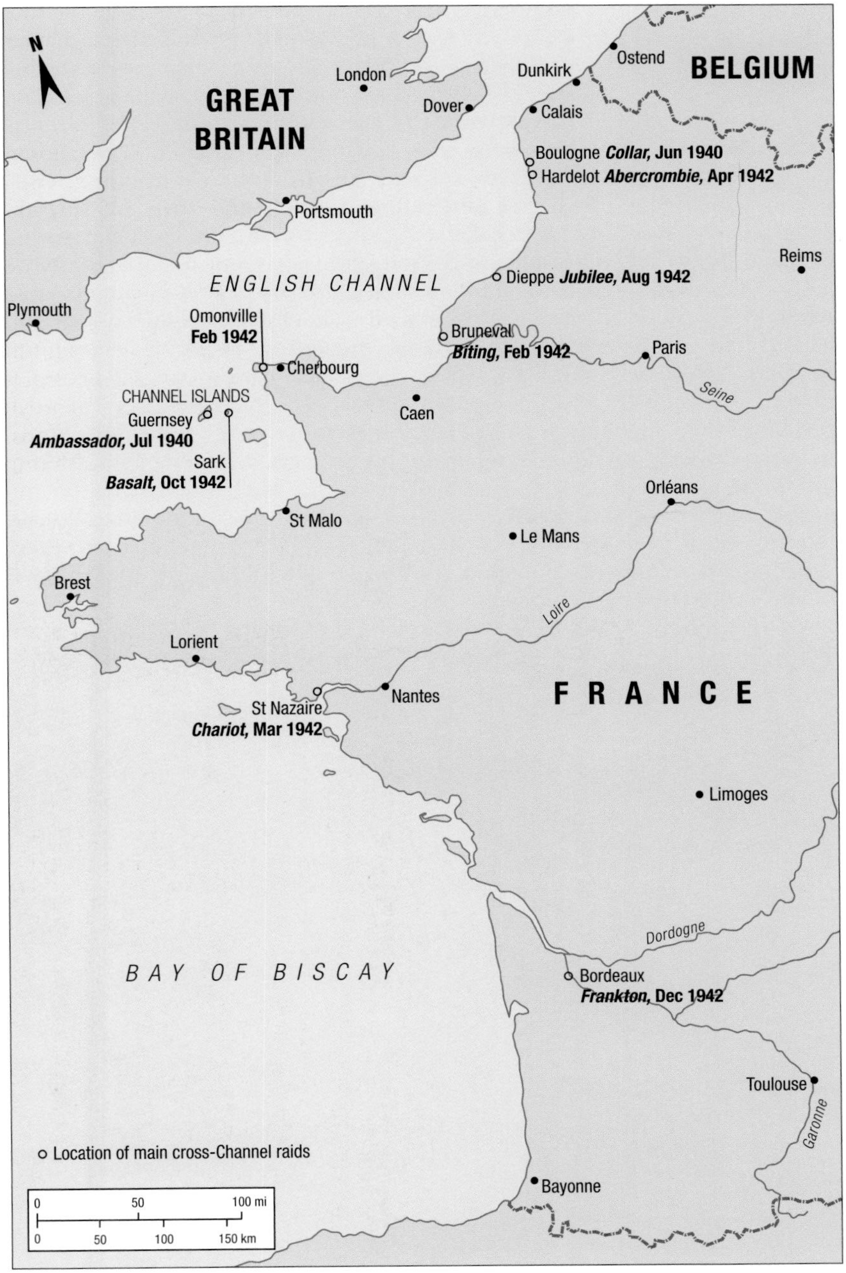
N
GREAT BRITAIN
London
Dover
Portsmouth
Plymouth
BELGIUM
Ostend
Dunkirk
Calais
Boulogne *Collar*, Jun 1940
Hardelot *Abercrombie*, Apr 1942
ENGLISH CHANNEL
Dieppe *Jubilee*, Aug 1942
Reims
Omonville Feb 1942
Cherbourg
Bruneval *Biting*, Feb 1942
Paris
Seine
CHANNEL ISLANDS
Guernsey
Ambassador, Jul 1940
Sark
Basalt, Oct 1942
Caen
Orléans
St Malo
Le Mans
Brest
Loire
Lorient
Nantes
FRANCE
St Nazaire
Chariot, Mar 1942
Limoges
Dordogne
BAY OF BISCAY
Bordeaux
Frankton, Dec 1942
Toulouse
Garonne
Bayonne
o Location of main cross-Channel raids
0 50 100 mi
0 50 100 150 km

The locations of the main cross-Channel Commando raids, together with the relevant operation names and dates.

A British Commando shares a cigarette with a US Army Ranger after returning from the Dieppe raid. (H22580)

dispositions, and terrain conditions for mounting further projected raids or major amphibious operations. Although other more specialized units, such as Combined Operations Pilotage Parties (technically part of the Special Service Brigade), took over the task of beach reconnaissance, collecting intelligence remained a key Commando mission.

The Commandos forming part of Special Service Brigade ably fulfilled their combat mission as a seaborne raiding force between 1940 and 1942. As the war progressed the perceived need for such operations, however, gradually disappeared. A major change occurred in the combat mission of the Commandos early in 1943 as a result: their role was now as lightly equipped assault infantry, specializing in spearheading large-scale opposed amphibious assaults and then participating in the fighting during the ensuing follow-up and consolidation phases. The former included seizing vital ground, neutralizing coastal batteries, guarding the flanks of landing beaches, and then fighting for extended periods alongside regular army units ashore. The participation of Commandos in the follow-up and consolidation phases of major amphibious landings proved increasingly important given the rapidly deteriorating manpower position in the UK. While small-scale raiding operations were still carried out where opportunity offered (including operations along the shoreline of Norway and Italy, Burma, and the Aegean), the Commandos increasingly took their place on the conventional battlefield for extended periods of time operating as part of larger formations. The unique skills honed in earlier raiding operations, moreover, meant their combat mission during follow-on operations included such diverse tasks as reconnaissance behind enemy lines, making opposed river crossings, and operating across difficult terrain, impassable by wheeled vehicles and heavy weapons. In these situations, their organization and specialized skills as highly trained light infantry could be fully exploited.

British Commandos from 3rd Commando Brigade wade ashore from a Royal Indian Navy Landing Craft during the Third Arakan campaign. (IND 4334)

Organization

Formation and early organization

The defence of the UK understandably formed the focus of the British Army's activities following the astonishing success of the German Blitzkrieg in May 1940. However, early in June 1940 the urgent necessity of hitting back at German-occupied Europe quickly grasped the attention of Winston Churchill, the Prime Minister. He wished to rebuild badly shaken British morale after the Fall of France, demonstrate a capacity to take the offensive, and show the public and the free world that Britain remained undefeated. In a minute addressed to the Chiefs of Staff written on 3 June 1940, he urged:

> The completely defensive habit of mind, which has ruined the French, must not be allowed to ruin all our initiative. It is of the highest consequence to keep the largest number of German forces all along the coasts of the countries that have been conquered, and we should immediately set to work to organise raiding forces on these coasts where the population is friendly.

Similarly on 5 June Churchill directed:

> Enterprises must be prepared with specially trained troops of the hunter class who can develop a reign of terror down the enemy coast ... I look to the Chiefs of Staff to propose measures for a ceaseless offensive against the whole German occupied coastline, leaving a trail of corpses behind.[2]

These bold, daring and highly imaginative ideas were carefully considered by the Chiefs of Staff at a meeting held on 6 June, with initial discussion directed towards building up a 'striking force' based upon an existing regular formation. Given the paramount necessity of organizing conventional units and formations for the defence of the UK, however, this idea proved stillborn. On 10 June Lt Col Dudley Clarke (a South African by birth), serving as Military Assistant to Lt Gen Sir John Dill (the newly appointed Chief of the Imperial General Staff), drew up detailed proposals for a raiding force, basing his ideas on the small irregular bands of Boer Commandos who had employed guerrilla warfare so effectively against the much larger British Army during the Second Boer War (1899–1902), and on his own experiences during the 1936 Arab Rebellion. As he later admitted: 'Since the Commandos seemed the best exponent of guerrilla warfare which history could provide, it was presumably the best model we could adopt.' When presented to the Prime Minister (himself a veteran of the Boer War), his proposals for forming 'Commandos' and employing irregular fighting methods were greeted with great enthusiasm. Within days Clarke was appointed to head a new section of the secretariat of Military Operations – MO9 – at the War Office to organize 'uniformed raids'.

The initial concept underlying the purpose, formation and employment of these new Commandos was comprehensively described in a memorandum dated 13 June 1940 sent out by Maj Gen R.H. Dewing, the Director of Military Operations and Plans at the War Office, which dictated the organization and equipment of Commandos:

> The object of forming a commando is to collect together a number of individuals trained to fight independently as an irregular and not as a

formed military unit. For this reason a commando will have no unit equipment and need not necessarily have a fixed establishment. Any establishment that may be produced will be for the purposes of allotting appropriate ranks in the right proportions to each other.

Irregular operations will be initiated by the War Office. Each one must necessarily require different arms, equipment and methods, and the purpose of the commandos will be to produce whatever number of irregulars are required to carry out the operations. An officer will be appointed by the War Office to each separate operation and the troops detailed to carry it out will be armed and equipped for that operation only from central sources controlled by the War Office ...

When a commando is detailed by the War Office for some specific operation arms and equipment will be issued on the scale required, and the commando will be moved (usually by separate Troops) to the jumping off place for the operation. As a rule the operation will not take more than a few days, after which the commando would be returned to its original 'Home Town' where it will train and wait, probably for several weeks, before taking part in another operation. It will be seen from the above that there should be practically no administrative requirements on the Q side in the formation or operation of these commandos. The A side must of course be looked after, and for this purpose I am proposing to appoint an administrative officer to each Commando who will relieve the commando leader of paperwork. This administrative officer will have a permanent headquarters in the 'home town' of his commando.

The commando organization is really intended to provide no more than a pool of specialized soldiers from which irregular units of any size and type can be very quickly created to undertake any particular task.

The main characteristics of a commando in action are:
a) Capable only of operating independently for 24 hours;
b) Capable of very wide dispersion and individual action;
c) Not capable of resisting an attack or overcoming a defence of formed bodies of troops, i.e. specializing in tip and run tactics dependent for their success upon speed, ingenuity and dispersion.[3]

Order of battle, Army Commando, June 1940

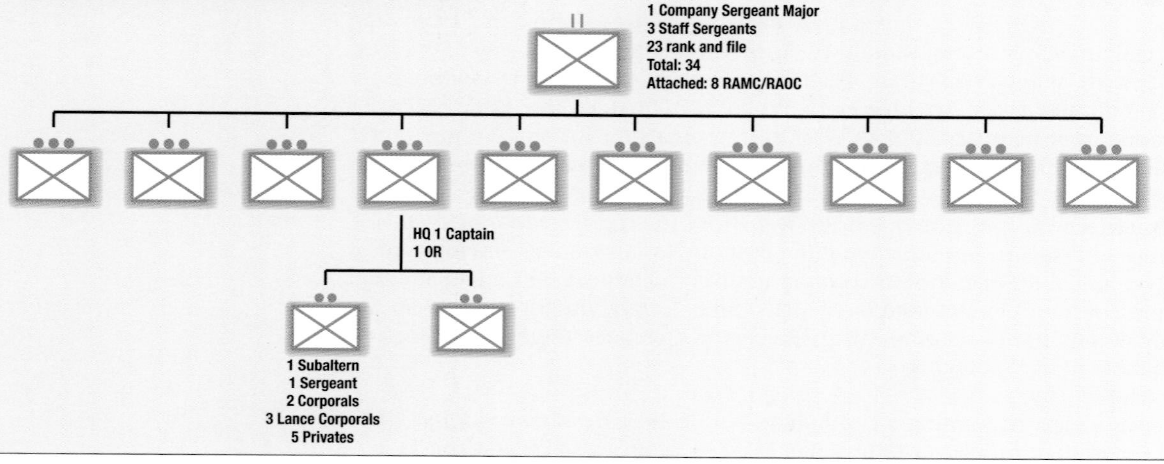
7 officers
1 Company Sergeant Major
3 Staff Sergeants
23 rank and file
Total: 34
Attached: 8 RAMC/RAOC
HQ 1 Captain
1 OR
1 Subaltern
1 Sergeant
2 Corporals
3 Lance Corporals
5 Privates

Lt Col Dudley Lister and Maj Robert Laycock with Polish, Dutch, Belgian, Norwegian and French officers of No. 10 (Inter-Allied) Commando. (H31039)

The formation and idea behind the Commandos, solely organized, trained and equipped for raiding, was revolutionary in many respects for the British Army and an experiment from start to finish. The Prime Minister's strong support and the drive and enthusiasm of those officers responsible for implementing the new scheme, however, injected a sense of urgency into getting the Commandos up and running with the minimum delay. When the idea of adapting and employing existing units for this highly specialized new role was abandoned, the War Office issued a call to arms on 9 June to units in Northern and Southern Commands calling for volunteers (a similar letter was disseminated to other Commands several days later) to join a new special force for 'mobile operations' and 'special service of a hazardous nature'. Despite lacking any real detail as to the conditions of service and role of this new force, volunteers of all ranks quickly answered the call to serve in these new units, to the immediate consternation of some regular officers who feared regular army units were being stripped of their best officers and men. They had some real grounds for concern. Undoubtedly many would have become officers and NCOs in due course if they had remained with their parent units. As one officer described:

> Commanding officers were to ensure that only the best were sent; they must be young, absolutely fit, able to drive motor vehicles, and unable to be seasick. It was a leap in the dark for absolutely nothing was said as to what they were to do, and in any case most regular officers make a point of never volunteering for anything.'[4]

A huge cross-section of men from every 'teeth' arm and service of the British Army – Regular, Territorial and reservists – came forward seeking action, adventure and escape from the humdrum of normal wartime military service. None of the picked volunteers that came forward were by any means 'supermen'. In the words of one distinguished Commando officer:

> The Commando volunteers of 1940 may have been rather special in their way – they were all picked volunteers. But they were far from regarding themselves as anything out of the ordinary. Few were of gigantic stature,

> and, until they had received their specialist training, few were exceptionally skilful in the martial arts. The great majority had never been under fire. They were just fed up with being told the Germans were supermen and that they themselves were 'wet'. And so they revolted against their age and went to war in a new spirit of dedicated ferocity.[5]

The new Commandos were raised with commendable speed from these volunteers during the summer of 1940, with powerful support emanating from Churchill. Each Command HQ in the United Kingdom (for administrative convenience given responsibility for forming either one or two Commandos) first selected suitable Officers Commanding from a pool of volunteers, who were then made responsible for selecting Troop Leaders (see table 1). These junior officers in turn were given a free hand and travelled around the country interviewing and in turn selecting suitable rank and file from NCOs and Other Ranks who had presented themselves for 'Special Service'. As a result, from the outset the new Commando was imbued with the enthusiasm, spirit and drive of individual COs and junior officers, who played a key role in 'setting the tone' for each unit. Indeed, it was the selfless and dedicated leadership of these men that did so much to shape the Commandos for the rest of the war and to achieve such impressive results. This 'rough and ready' system of recruiting in practice worked pretty well in terms of selecting suitable men. All those selected were seconded to the Commandos, retaining their own cap badges and remaining on the roll of their individual regiments for pay.

The war establishment of regular infantry battalions, equipped with MT and heavy weapons, was clearly inappropriate for carrying out raids without major modification. A new organization was hurriedly devised dictated by the highly specialized, sole task of carrying out short-lived hit-and-run raids lasting less than 24 hours before withdrawing to the UK. Since the scope of planned operations varied widely, the war establishment of these units was deliberately granted flexibility in terms of organization, equipment and training. A small HQ consisting of a lieutenant-colonel, a second in command, adjutant, medical officer, intelligence officer and an administrative officer, with a CSM, three staff sergeants and 23 ORs, as well as eight attached RAMC and RAOC personnel, led each unit in the field. Each Commando only had a total strength of approximately 500 officers and men, which was far lower than a normal infantry battalion. Each Commando was organized into ten 'Fighting Troops', led by a captain, each subdivided in turn into two sections led by a subaltern. As noted the Commandos were issued initially with the same scale of personal weapons – .38 revolvers, .303 Lee-Enfield rifles, Thompson sub-machine guns

Table 1: responsibility for formation of early Commandos

No. 1 Commando	Formed from disbanded Independent Companies
No. 2 Commando	Raised from volunteers from all Commands
No. 3 Commando	Southern Command
No. 4 Commando	Southern Command
No. 5 Commando	Western Command
No. 6 Commando	Western Command
No. 7 Commando	Eastern Command
No. 8 Commando	Eastern Command (in reality from London District and the Household Division.)
No. 9 Commando	Scottish Command
No. 11 Commando	Scottish Command
No. 10 Commando	Northern Command

and Bren light machine guns – and equipment as per the rest of the British military, with any other special equipment required for a specific operation or training issued as and when required from a central reserve. Apart from Boyes 0.55in. AT rifles, heavy weapons were marked by their absence, since Commandos were not expected either to mount a protracted defence or overcome defences held by formed bodies of troops. Other than an officer tasked with overseeing troops living in civilian billets, each unit had only a small administrative tail, since they would operate from a secure, fixed base in the UK, with each man carrying solely what was required on operations. The only vehicles provided were those for day-to-day use while the unit was in the UK, with none intended to accompany a unit on operations.

Several specialized sub-units were also raised as part of some Commandos during 1940 at the discretion of individual COs. A special section – dubbed 101 Troop – was formed in No. 6 Commando in July 1940 equipped with Folboat canoes to carry out sea raiding. Similarly, under the command of Lieutenant Roger Courtney, No. 8 Commando raised a Folboat section for sabotaging ships in harbour. Both were to form the basis of later Special Boat Section units.

The initial progress made in recruiting, organizing and training the new Commandos from scratch was mixed during the summer of 1940, hampered by chronic shortages of arms and equipment. Many early volunteers, moreover, were found unsuitable and suffered the ultimate ignominy for a Commando recruit of being 'RTUed' (Returned to Unit). Other problems caused delay. The formation of No. 1 Commando was delayed, for example, as the operational Independent Companies (from which it was to draw its manpower) remained in place due to the threat of imminent German invasion. Similarly it took time for No. 2 Commando, formed as a parachute unit, to find and recruit sufficient volunteers from units scattered all over the UK. Only No. 10 Commando failed to form, as insufficient volunteers from Northern Command were forthcoming; this title was left temporarily vacant. A No. 12 Commando was also raised slightly later than the others in Northern Ireland from local resources, but only had an initial strength of 250 men (half that of the others).

The Prime Minister's impatience and the lack of readiness of nearly all the new Commandos for combat meant ironically that the first 'Commando' raid of World War II was entrusted to an Independent Company. Raised from volunteers from 2nd Line Territorial Army Divisions in April 1940 by MI(R) as 'guerrilla companies' specifically for use in Norway following the German invasion, each of the ten units initially created consisted of 21 officers and 268 ORs, who had been trained to fight as distinct self-contained units. Within days five Independent Companies were loaded aboard ship and committed to action in central Norway. By 10 June all had returned to UK in considerable disarray following the disastrous Norwegian campaign. The remaining five Independent Companies fortunately never the left the UK and remained under training in the Glasgow area before carrying out anti-invasion duties. A new No. 11 Independent Company, commanded by Maj Ronnie Tod, had formed on 14 June 1940 for 'special operations' from volunteers from the other companies in Scotland. With a strength of 25 officers and 350 ORs it moved to Southampton and carried out the first cross-Channel raid on 24 June 1940 near Boulogne. On the night of 24/25 June, using RAF crash boats based at Dover, Ramsgate and Newhaven, No. 11 Independent Company landed small parties near Hardelot, Stella Plage and Berck at night to reconnoitre and capture German prisoners. Operation *Collar* met with mixed success and the only casualty suffered was that of Lt Col Dudley Clarke, who was slightly wounded. A similar debacle took place several weeks later during Operation *Ambassador*, involving 140 men drawn from No. 11 Independent Company and one troop of No. 3 Commando, which due to the large number of regulars in its ranks was the first true Commando to be ready for combat (see the *Combat operations* chapter).

The formation of the Special Service Brigade

The initial organization adopted by Commando units in June 1940 proved short-lived, as the pressure mounted to rationalize the multitude of organizations in the UK responsible for special operations. A new Special Service Brigade, commanded by Brig Charles Haydon (a highly decorated Irish Guardsman), was formed in November 1940 by the simple expedient of merging the Commandos with existing Independent Companies. Its primary function was still raiding operations and not home defence. This highly experimental new unit ultimately consisted of five 'Special Service Battalions', each having two Special Service Companies. In turn each had ten troops or platoons of 50 men that were divided into two sections and again each into two sub-sections. A further change in organization so soon after units had been raised did not go down well with officers and men. As Major Bill Copland, former i/c No. 4 Independent Company, wrote:

Men of No. 1 Commando climb out of an ALC after a Combined Operations exercise on the Isle of Wight. (H20393)

Order of battle, Special Service Brigade, November 1940

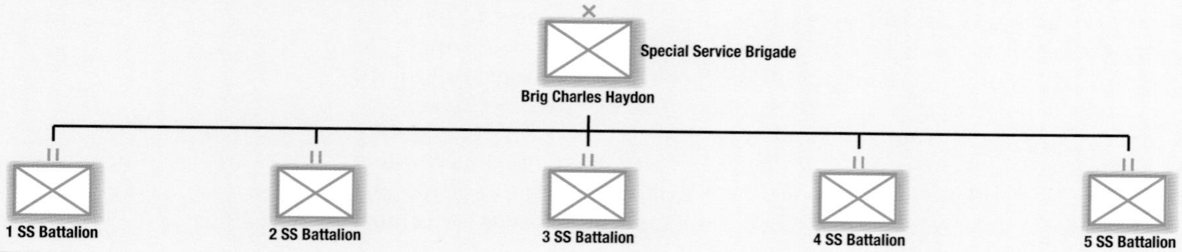
Special Service Brigade
Brig Charles Haydon
1 SS Battalion
2 SS Battalion
3 SS Battalion
4 SS Battalion
5 SS Battalion

> And so into another new organization goes the cream of the Independent Companies which were born in a muddle, suffered in the chaos of Norway, wasted months of valuable time at home when tasks which other troops botched could have been done well by them.[6]

Not all the Commandos, however, automatically became part of the Special Service Brigade. No. 2 Commando, for example, was soon re-designated 11 Special Air Service Battalion, before eventually becoming 1st Parachute Battalion and then the Parachute Regiment. Subsequently a new No. 2 Commando was formed under Lt Col Charles Newman from a fresh batch of volunteers. No. 12 Commando also remained temporarily outside the Special Service Battalion organization in Northern Ireland.

Table 2: the composition of Special Service Battalions, November 1940

1st Special Service Battalion	Formed from Nos. 1, 2, 3, 4, 5, 8 and 9 Independent Companies
2nd Special Service Battalion	Nos. 6 and 7 Independent Companies and Nos. 9 and 11 Commandos
3rd Special Service Battalion	No. 4 and No. 7 Commandos
4th Special Service Battalion	No. 3 and No. 8 Commandos
5th Special Service Battalion	No. 5 and No. 6 Commandos

Order of battle, Special Service Battalion, November 1940

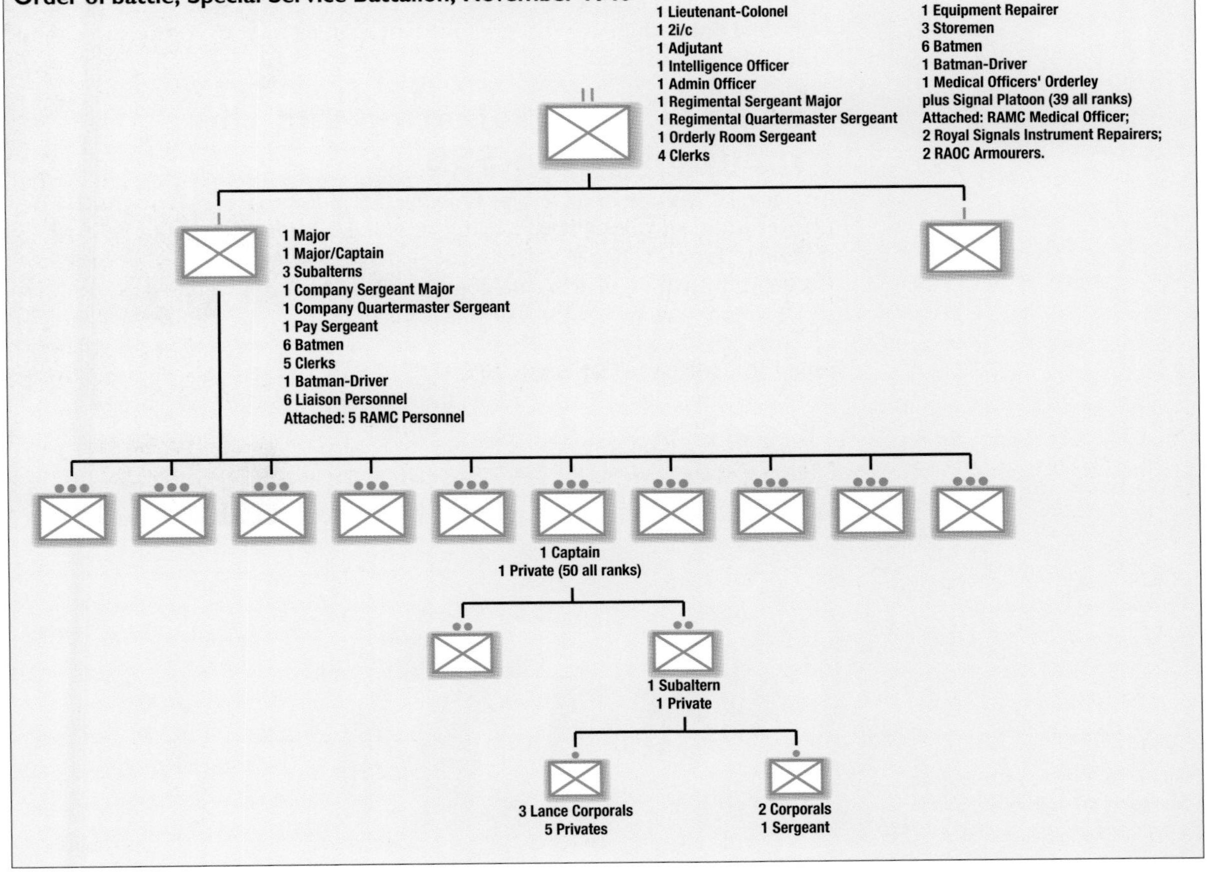
1 Lieutenant-Colonel
1 2i/c
1 Adjutant
1 Intelligence Officer
1 Admin Officer
1 Regimental Sergeant Major
1 Regimental Quartermaster Sergeant
1 Orderly Room Sergeant
4 Clerks
1 Equipment Repairer
3 Storemen
6 Batmen
1 Batman-Driver
1 Medical Officers' Orderley
plus Signal Platoon (39 all ranks)
Attached: RAMC Medical Officer;
2 Royal Signals Instrument Repairers;
2 RAOC Armourers.
1 Major
1 Major/Captain
3 Subalterns
1 Company Sergeant Major
1 Company Quartermaster Sergeant
1 Pay Sergeant
6 Batmen
5 Clerks
1 Batman-Driver
6 Liaison Personnel
Attached: 5 RAMC Personnel
1 Captain
1 Private (50 all ranks)
1 Subaltern
1 Private
3 Lance Corporals
5 Privates
2 Corporals
1 Sergeant

The Special Service Battalion war establishment, however, did not prove a success. As early as 1 February 1941 Brig Charles Hayden strongly recommended a reversion to the original idea of small Commandos on the grounds that the battalion concept had proved extremely unpopular. Indeed, it had caused open resentment amongst those who had raised the Commandos and amongst the men who had joined them. Perhaps most notably, the individualistic CO of No. 3 Commando had even refused to recognize the existence of the new Special Service Battalion of which his unit formed a part, and had retained the title Commando in all official correspondence. Many set against the abbreviated title – 'SS' – given its unfortunate association with German units having the same initials. Several practical reasons also influenced this decision. The large and unwieldy Special Service battalions (fielding 77 officers and 1,053 Other Ranks) proved extremely difficult to command and control during training, given that each unit had so few staff officers or vehicles. It also proved extremely difficult to administer, particularly when finding sufficient billets for all officers and men in a given area. Furthermore, the large size of the Special Service battalion and its subunits had tactical and operational implications for raiding, since it simply did not match the capacity of the small number of available assault ships. Neither the Glen-type (HMS *Glenearn*, HMS *Glenroy*, and HMS *Glengyle*) landing ships, merchantmen fitted with davits from which Assault Landing Craft were lowered, or Dutch type landing ships (HMS *Beatrix*, HMS *Prince Albert* and HMS *Princess Emma*), formerly passenger steamers, could carry a complete battalion in a single lift. As a result each Special Service Battalion had to be subdivided into smaller groups to fit aboard ship, thereby severely complicating command and control. It was impossible to fit a company, moreover, into a single Armoured Landing Craft (ALC). Finally, the size of each battalion meant it was highly unlikely a complete unit would ever be employed on a single task, making a reversion to a small basic unit ideal.

The 1941 reorganization and the expansion of the SSB

The Special Service Brigade was reorganized in February 1941, with the new organization and designation being adopted while the Lofoten raid was in progress. Various changes were also made in the organization of individual Commandos with a view to making them easier to command and control and more suited to available ships and landing craft.

The individual Commando were reorganized, in accordance with a new war establishment issued in February 1941, into an HQ with six Fighting Troops (instead of ten, as before). Each Fighting Troop now had a total strength of

Men of No. 3 (Army) Commando undergoing ski training at Killin in Perthshire, Scotland, 22 March 1942. (H18098)

Commando War Establishment, 24 February 1941

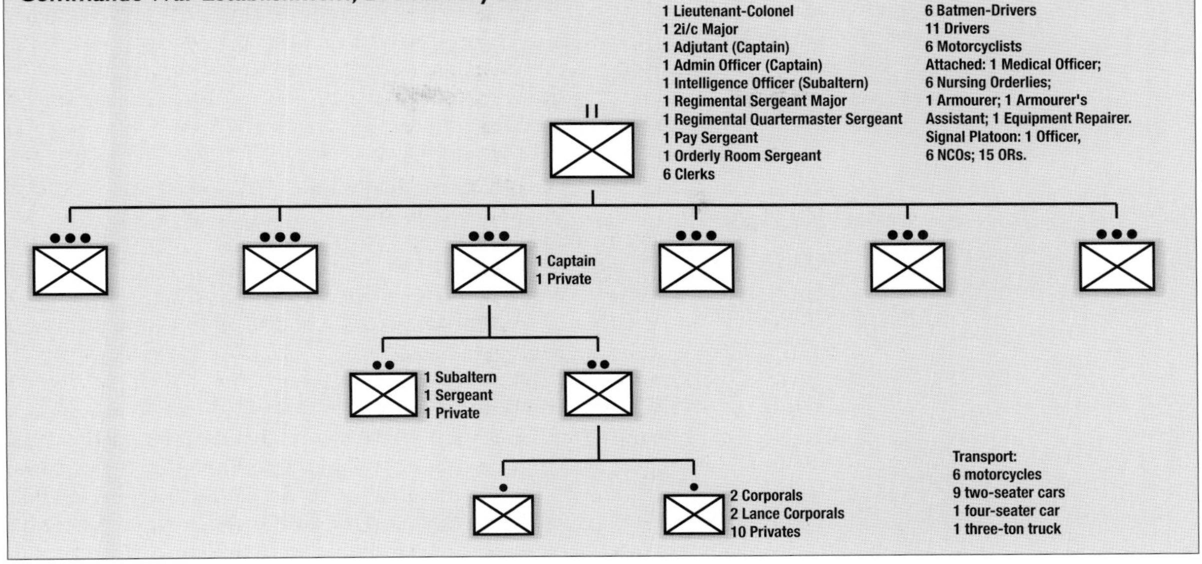
1 Lieutenant-Colonel
1 2i/c Major
1 Adjutant (Captain)
1 Admin Officer (Captain)
1 Intelligence Officer (Subaltern)
1 Regimental Sergeant Major
1 Regimental Quartermaster Sergeant
1 Pay Sergeant
1 Orderly Room Sergeant
6 Clerks
6 Batmen-Drivers
11 Drivers
6 Motorcyclists
Attached: 1 Medical Officer;
6 Nursing Orderlies;
1 Armourer; 1 Armourer's
Assistant; 1 Equipment Repairer.
Signal Platoon: 1 Officer,
6 NCOs; 15 ORs.
1 Captain
1 Private
1 Subaltern
1 Sergeant
1 Private
2 Corporals
2 Lance Corporals
10 Privates
Transport:
6 motorcycles
9 two-seater cars
1 four-seater car
1 three-ton truck

Special Service Brigade, March 1941

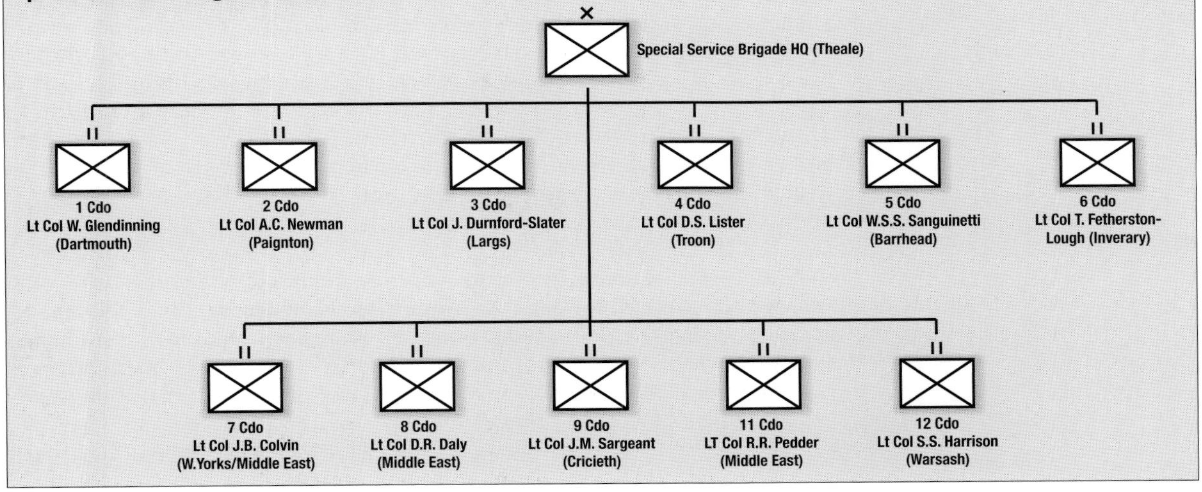
Special Service Brigade HQ (Theale)
1 Cdo
Lt Col W. Glendinning
(Dartmouth)
2 Cdo
Lt Col A.C. Newman
(Paignton)
3 Cdo
Lt Col J. Durnford-Slater
(Largs)
4 Cdo
Lt Col D.S. Lister
(Troon)
5 Cdo
Lt Col W.S.S. Sanguinetti
(Barrhead)
6 Cdo
Lt Col T. Fetherston-
Lough (Inverary)
7 Cdo
Lt Col J.B. Colvin
(W.Yorks/Middle East)
8 Cdo
Lt Col D.R. Daly
(Middle East)
9 Cdo
Lt Col J.M. Sargeant
(Cricieth)
11 Cdo
LT Col R.R. Pedder
(Middle East)
12 Cdo
Lt Col S.S. Harrison
(Warsash)

three officers and 62 ORs, so that each would fit neatly into two Assault Landing Craft, leaving space free for five additional attached personnel. Two complete Commandos would now fit aboard a Glen-type landing ship and a single one into each Dutch type. Moreover, this reduction in the total number of officers and men in a Commando and in the number of Troops that made them up, made them far easier to command and control on operations under cover of night and ensured all troops could travel in one ship. A reduction in the strength of each Commando had another unintended benefit, in providing a relatively painless way of ridding units of unwanted officers, NCOs, and men. Otherwise no changes were made in the amount of supporting weapons allocated to each Commando. The transport allocated to each Commando also remained on just an administrative basis only with six motorcycles, six motorcycle combinations, one car, two 15cwt trucks, and one 3-ton lorry per Commando. None was intended to accompany the unit on active service; they were provided purely for administrative and training purposes.

Table 3: order of battle of the Special Service Brigade, March 1941	
No. 1 Special Service Battalion	No. 1 Commando
	No. 2 Commando
No. 2 Special Service Battalion	No. 9 Commando
No. 3 Special Service Battalion	No. 4 Commando
No. 4 Special Service Battalion	No. 3 Commando
No. 5 Special Service Battalion	No. 5 Commando
	No. 6 Commando
No. 12 Commando	*(separate from bns; based in N. Ireland)*

The Commandos in the Middle East

The formation of the Commandos in the UK was mirrored during 1940 by the creation of a similar, albeit much smaller, organization in the Middle East, when the War Office ordered GHQ Middle East Land Forces (MELF) to follow its lead, even though the two organizations were largely separate from each other. This was overseen by the MI(R) Branch of GHQ Middle East, commanded by Col Adrian Simpson, which had overall responsibility for organizing and overseeing the raising and training of irregular forces. Although hampered by acute shortages of equipment in theatre, volunteers flooded in to form these units. Under the command of Lt Col George Young, No. 50 Commando was formed in August 1940 at Geneifa from volunteers from units in the Middle East, as well as a small contingent of Spanish Civil War veterans who had escaped to Palestine following the fall of France. This unit had a provisional establishment of HQ and three troops, each of four sections. The latter consisted of one officer and 25 NCOs and men. Each Commando had a total strength of 371 all ranks, with an RAMC doctor and three orderlies, RAOC armourer and two interpreters attached. No. 51 Commando was raised in October 1940 under the command of Lt Col Henry Cator, with a nucleus provided by 300 Palestinians drawn from the former No. 1 Palestinian Company of the Auxiliary Military Pioneer Corps. A third Commando – No. 52 Commando – followed on 2 November, commanded by Lt Col Fox-Davies, with its manpower provided by volunteers from British units in theatre. It suffered from having few suitable men, however, as many canny COs took the opportunity to 'volunteer' their malcontents and

Provisional establishment of Middle East Commando, July 1940

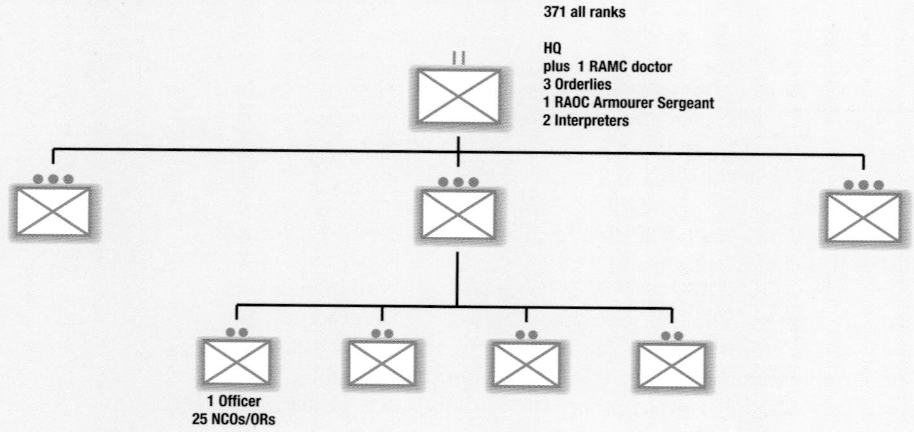
371 all ranks
HQ
plus 1 RAMC doctor
3 Orderlies
1 RAOC Armourer Sergeant
2 Interpreters
1 Officer
25 NCOs/ORs

shirkers. A Middle East Commando Depot was also formed in mid December 1940 and was formally established on 25 January, responsible for training and supplying individual reinforcements for the three Commandos in theatre.

These units suffered initial frustrations in terms of organization and equipment, but then quickly found themselves heavily embroiled in sustained combat operations, unlike those in the UK, in North Africa, East Africa and Crete. Few units, however, were used in their correct role.

The greatest change in the order of battle of the Middle East Commandos occurred in March 1941 when a large force of Commandos – comprising Nos. 7, 8, and 11 (Scottish) Commandos, a troop of No. 3 Commando, and a Folboat section (soon renamed No. 1 SBS) – was despatched from the UK, commanded by Colonel Robert Laycock, aboard HMS *Glenearn*, HMS *Glenroy* and HMS

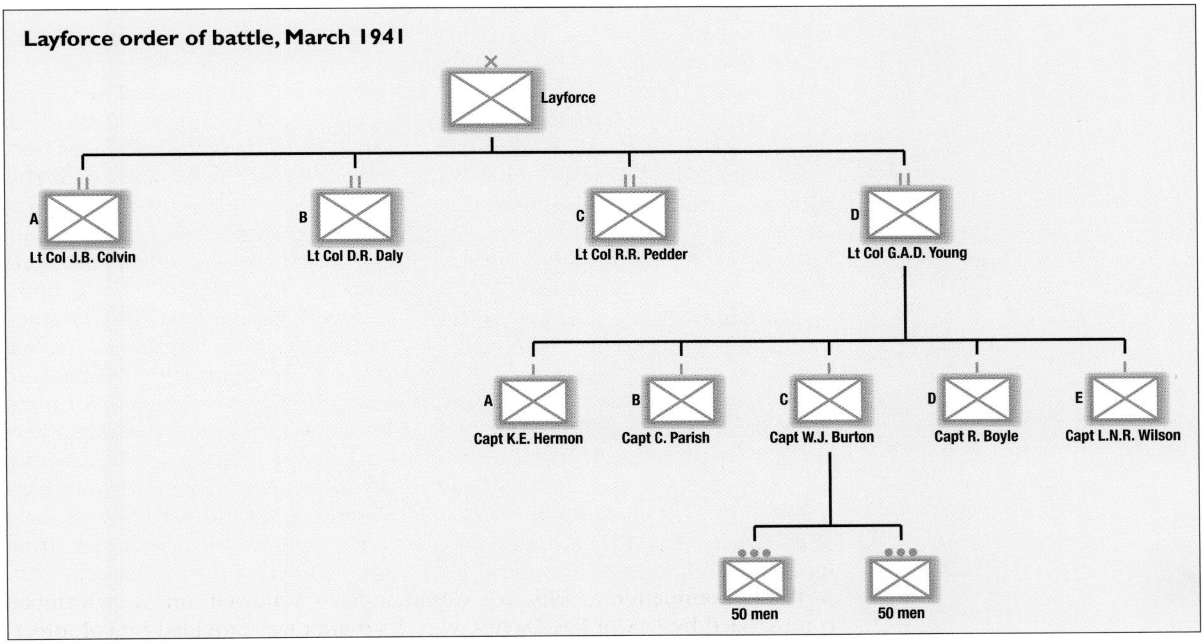
Layforce order of battle, March 1941
Layforce
A
Lt Col J.B. Colvin
B
Lt Col D.R. Daly
C
Lt Col R.R. Pedder
D
Lt Col G.A.D. Young
A
Capt K.E. Hermon
B
Capt C. Parish
C
Capt W.J. Burton
D
Capt R. Boyle
E
Capt L.N.R. Wilson
50 men
50 men

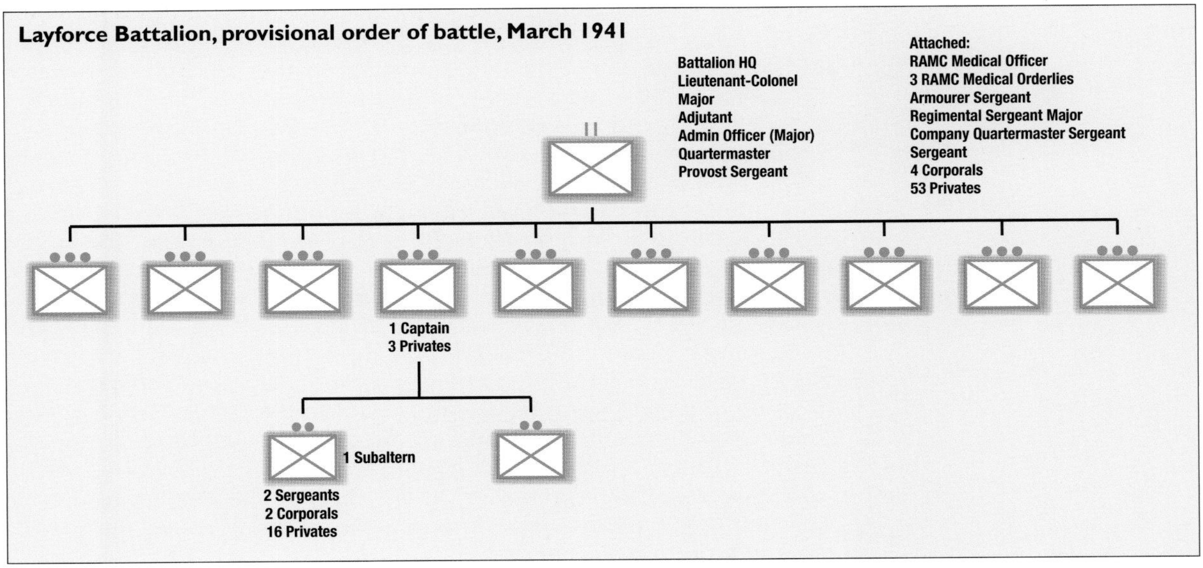
Layforce Battalion, provisional order of battle, March 1941
Battalion HQ
Lieutenant-Colonel
Major
Adjutant
Admin Officer (Major)
Quartermaster
Provost Sergeant
Attached:
RAMC Medical Officer
3 RAMC Medical Orderlies
Armourer Sergeant
Regimental Sergeant Major
Company Quartermaster Sergeant
Sergeant
4 Corporals
53 Privates
1 Captain
3 Privates
1 Subaltern
2 Sergeants
2 Corporals
16 Privates

Glengyle specifically for Operation *Cordite* (the capture of the island of Rhodes). The under-strength No. 50 and 52 Commandos were amalgamated in March 1941 (already on a smaller establishment than those from the UK) when Force Z arrived at Geneifa and joined them. To provide secrecy the term Commando was deliberately not used as part of this force's title, which instead was simply rechristened Layforce. It consisted of four 'battalions', in an attempt to delete all references to the Commandos, but unlike a regular formation of this size lacked any transport or supporting arms.

The rapidly deteriorating overall military position in the Middle East meant Layforce was never employed in a specialized role as intended. Although several raids were mounted along the North African littoral – notably at Bardia on the night of 19/20 April – the campaigns in North Africa and Greece diverted the shipping required for amphibious operations. Layforce was rapidly broken up and sucked into the fighting in North Africa and Crete in April where it was employed in a conventional role, despite having no heavy weapons and little appropriate training. A heavy penalty was paid by the Commandos for committing these specialist troops to battle without adequate heavy supporting weapons and in such a role. Both A and D Battalions of Layforce suffered heavily while conducting a series of rearguard actions across the island and the lion's share of the men went into German captivity. Although two battalions remained intact, Layforce's days were numbered. For a short while B Battalion carried out raids in North Africa, while C Battalion, diverted from garrison duty in Cyprus, suffered heavy losses in the Litani River landing during the invasion of Vichy French Syria.

The remnants of Layforce and No. 51 ME Commando were disbanded during the summer on the orders of FM Wavell and his successor Gen Sir Claude Auchinleck, largely on account of the chronic shortages of manpower in the Middle East, lack of assault shipping, and the impossibility of mounting further amphibious operations in the short term. On 15 July Layforce formally ceased to exist, although elements of it lived on into the autumn, as well as No. 51 Commando and the Commando Depot. The majority of survivors were returned to their parent units or else were absorbed into the multitude of other elite units such as the SAS and SBS which were eventually incorporated into the Raiding Force, Middle East or else served in the Far East.

However, the Commandos in the Middle East were briefly resurrected on the express orders of an infuriated Winston Churchill, who fervently believed these highly specialized units had been misused and frittered away in the theatre. A new Middle East Commando, initially commanded by Laycock and then Lt Col J.M. Graham, was formed; it was very different from its predecessors. It took over the Geneifa Depot and initially absorbed the remnants of Layforce, elements of 51 ME Commando (recently arrived back in Egypt), L Detachment of the newly formed Special Air Service, and personnel from the Special Boat Section. In November 1941 its No. 3 Troop (still calling itself No. 11 Commando) carried out a famous, abortive raid on Gen Erwin Rommel's suspected HQ at Beda Littoria, with most of its men being killed or captured. Both the SAS and SBS soon departed, however, with the bulk of the Middle East Commando coming under control of the SOE, Middle East and Balkans. A 'turf war' between the HQ of 8th Army and SOE over the use of Middle East Commando occurred as the overall military situation deteriorated, with the result that it was employed in a very different role from the one originally intended when it was reformed. Indeed, the title 'Commando' was simply retained as a cover and to satisfy Churchill's demands for such a unit in the Middle East. Following further reorganization into squadrons, the unit was re-titled the 1st Special Service Regiment in April 1942, to emphasize its 'special' as opposed to 'raiding' role, effectively destroying the last vestiges of its Commando identity. Unsurprisingly, the short-lived Middle East Commando never had the esprit de corps and cohesion of its predecessors.

The growth of the SSB: Royal Marine, Inter-Allied, and other new Commandos

The strength of the Special Service Brigade in the UK was steadily augmented during the early war years as the scale, tempo and success of Commando operations increased.

The first major change in the order of battle of the Special Service Brigade was the centralization of Commando training. To date the CO of each Commando had been primarily responsible for training his officers, NCOs and men. While a generally effective system, it had caused a marked variation in standards of training and instruction between units as well as greatly complicated the 'passing on' of the latest experience of combat operations. To remedy these problems a new Commando Depot opened at Achnacarry in Scotland in February 1942 where all volunteers, sub-units and new units henceforth carried out a period of intensive Commando training before joining an operation unit or formation. (See the *Doctrine and training* chapter for a detailed discussion of the role of Achnacarry).

A newly raised Royal Marine Commando strengthened the frontline fighting strength of the Special Service Brigade in February 1942. Early in 1942 volunteers were called for from units of the Royal Marine Division, which had remained ashore (apart from the Dakar Expedition) since the outbreak of war and formed a ready reserve of manpower, to form 'The Royal Marine Commando' (later redesignated simply as 'A Commando'). These men, primarily 'Hostilities Only' Royal Marines, assembled at Deal North Barracks on 14 February and, under the command of Lt Col Joseph Picton-Phillips, underwent intensive training. This new development in the history of the

Lt Col Charles Vaughan inspects French Commandos undergoing training at Achnacarry, Bastille Day, July 1943. (H31439)

No. 10 (Inter-Allied) Commando, outline order of battle, 1944–45

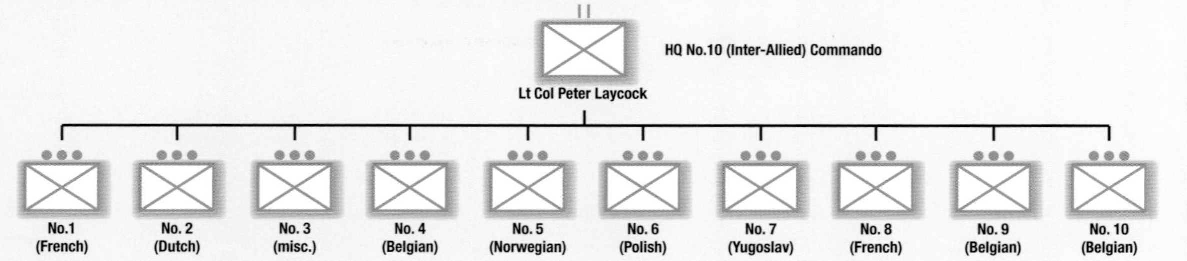
HQ No.10 (Inter-Allied) Commando
Lt Col Peter Laycock
No.1 (French)
No. 2 (Dutch)
No. 3 (misc.)
No. 4 (Belgian)
No. 5 (Norwegian)
No. 6 (Polish)
No. 7 (Yugoslav)
No. 8 (French)
No. 9 (Belgian)
No. 10 (Belgian)

No. 30 Commando (Special Engineering Unit) order of battle, 26 March 1943

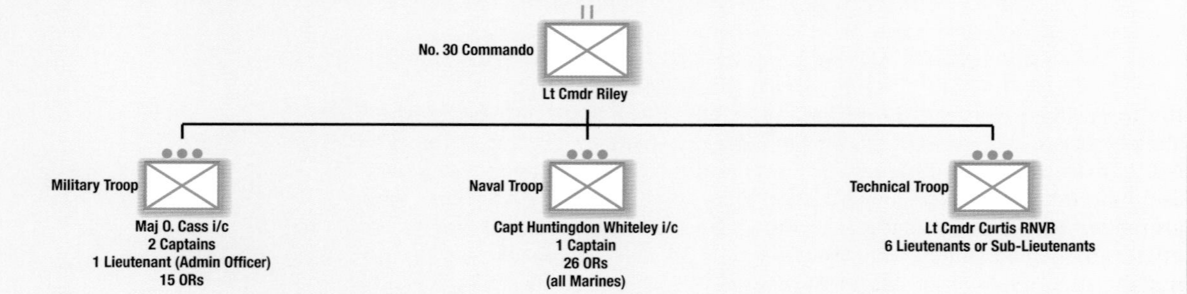
No. 30 Commando
Lt Cmdr Riley
Military Troop
Maj O. Cass i/c
2 Captains
1 Lieutenant (Admin Officer)
15 ORs
Naval Troop
Capt Huntingdon Whiteley i/c
1 Captain
26 ORs
(all Marines)
Technical Troop
Lt Cmdr Curtis RNVR
6 Lieutenants or Sub-Lieutenants

Commandos was by no means popular. Indeed, it met strong opposition from within the existing Army Commandos, wary of another service intruding into their domain, and from within the Corps of Royal Marines itself by those opposed to use of the corps in a manner so divorced from its normal shipboard role. Unlike other Commandos it was initially organized on a company basis. Following a period of intensive training and weeding out of unsuitable men, including time at the Commando Depot at Achnacarry, the unit had its baptism of fire during the disastrous Dieppe raid, after which in October 1942 it was re-titled 40 (Royal Marine) Commando.

A second Royal Marine Commando joined the Special Service Brigade in October 1942; instead of calling for volunteers, it was created by turning the existing 8th Royal Marine Battalion into a Commando unit. This was the source of another abiding criticism levelled by the Army Commandos at the Royal Marines, namely that they were 'pressed men' and not volunteers like their predecessors. B (RM) Commando, initially commanded by Lt Col O.H. Phibbs, quickly formed and joined A Commando on the Isle of Wight where it was later renamed No. 41 (Royal Marine) Commando. A frenzied period of weeding out was followed by intensive training for their new specialized role.

The order of battle of the Special Service Brigade was increased during 1942 by other various highly specialized units. Its strength was also augmented early in 1942 by a new highly experimental Inter-Allied Commando, recruited from men of various nationalities who had escaped from occupied Europe, whose language skills and local knowledge were judged ideal for raiding operations. No. 10 (Inter-Allied) Commando formally came into existence on 2 July 1942, was allocated the still-vacant title of No. 10 Commando (since Northern Command had failed to find sufficient volunteers), and was billeted in Wales. It was something of an experiment. Under the command of Lt Col Dudley Lister, only its HQ troop consisted entirely of British personnel. It incorporated an existing French *1er Compagnie Fusilier Marin*, which became No. 1 Troop of

Special Service Brigade order of battle, 1941–43

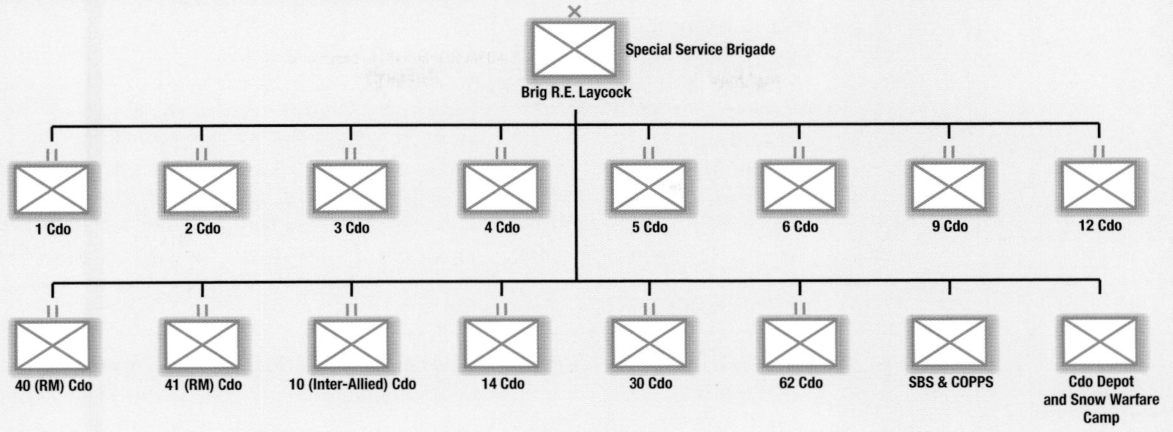
Special Service Brigade
Brig R.E. Laycock
1 Cdo
2 Cdo
3 Cdo
4 Cdo
5 Cdo
6 Cdo
9 Cdo
12 Cdo
40 (RM) Cdo
41 (RM) Cdo
10 (Inter-Allied) Cdo
14 Cdo
30 Cdo
62 Cdo
SBS & COPPS
Cdo Depot and Snow Warfare Camp

the Inter-Allied Commando, and was joined by a free Dutch troop that had already passed through the Commando Depot at Achnacarry, which became No. 2 Troop. Under conditions of extreme secrecy, X Troop – rather confusingly and inaccurately known as No. 3 (Miscellaneous) or the English troop – was also raised in July 1942 made up from enemy aliens, with its CO and several officers the only British members. It was undoubtedly one of the strangest, if not the strangest, sub-unit to serve in the British Army during World War II, being recruited from German and Austrian nationals, as well as German-speaking Czechs, Danes, Hungarians and a Russian and Rumanian, united in their opposition to the Nazi regime and who had volunteered from the Alien Companies of the Pioneer Corps or who had been working with Military Intelligence at the War Office. A No. 4 Belgian troop later joined the Commando followed by a No. 5 troop of Norwegians. The Polish or No. 6 was the last to join and consisted of five officers and 87 ORs. No. 10 (IA) Commando first saw action at Dieppe on 19 August 1942. This polyglot unit, steadily augmented in strength, served with distinction throughout the rest of the war, providing individuals, sub-units and complete troops for both clandestine and other more conventional specialized tasks.

The specialized task of intelligence gathering in the immediate wake of advancing troops was facilitated by the formation of another new unit under the umbrella of the Special Service Brigade. No. 30 Commando proved a unique addition, whose task was to operate alongside or in advance of forward combat units to seize documents or other material from captured enemy HQs or other facilities. Under the name of the Special Engineering Unit, it formed on 3 September 1942 under the Chief of Combined Operations. It consisted of three troops: No. 33 (Royal Marine), No. 34 (Army) and No. 36 (RN or Technical). Each had an establishment of two officers and 20 ORs, with the Army troop having only 12 ORs. While the first two came under the command of the Special Service Brigade No. 36 (RN) Troop was retained under RN control. Training covered general Commando skills as well as those required for its highly specialized role. It made its operational debut during the *Torch* landings in North Africa and played a major role throughout the rest of the war.

The Special Service Brigade now also nominally commanded No. 62 Commando. This was the cover name given to the Small Scale Raiding Force (SSRF) run jointly by the Special Operations Executive (SOE) and Combined Operations HQ. Originally formed in March 1942 at Mountbatten's direct request, this small unit (incorporating the existing Maid Honor Force that had assisted SOE with cross-Channel operations) consisted of 50 men from the

Commandos, intended as an 'amphibious sabotage force'. While administered and financed by SOE, it came under CCO's operational control. Equipped with two large motor launches it began carrying out a series of successful minor operations along the French coast and Channel Islands on behalf of the CCO in August, and its strength was gradually increased. A clash of interests between Combined Operations, SOE, SIS, and the Admiralty led to the SSRF's eventual disbandment in 1943.

The final addition to the fighting part of the Special Service Brigade was a new No. 14 Commando, raised in October 1942 at Lord Mountbatten's express request. It was to meet the demand for further raids in Norway, where activity had been limited since the Vaagso raid. In a minute to the Chiefs of Staff written on 5 November, he urged that further operations be mounted during the inhospitable Norwegian winter:

> It will be appreciated that the success of this type of operation is dependent upon the personnel being selected having considerable skill and experience in living and operating under conditions of extreme cold. Provided they are thoroughly skilled, particularly as skiers, operations which would not otherwise be feasible in winter could be carried out with every chance of success.[7]

Under the command of Lt Col E.A.M. Wedderburn, this highly specialized new unit was organized into two fighting troops: No. 1 (Boating) Troop, which had 9 officers and 18 ORs and specialized in small boat operations; and No. 2, which had six officers and 22 ORs as cross-country skiing specialists. Its ranks also included some Canadians, Norwegians, and members of the RNVR. This experimental Commando did not prove successful in practice and No. 1 (Boating) Troop was quickly disbanded, followed soon after by the rest of the unit.

Men of No. 1 Commando returning after a raid at St Cecily on the French coast, June 1942. (H20353)

The April 1943 expansion of and changes to the SSB

The lessons learnt by the Special Service Brigade during Operation *Torch* (the invasion of North Africa) and the ensuing fighting culminating in the destruction of Axis forces in Tunisia led to further changes in the Commando order of battle. Planning for the invasion of Sicily and later Italy, moreover, further reinforced this trend with the Commandos being employed in far greater numbers and on a far wider scale both during the assault and subsequent fighting ashore, in a role very different from that originally envisaged. A new type of war was clearly beginning for the men of the Special Service Brigade.

The background to this fundamental change in the size and combat mission of the elite Commandos merits much closer examination. During 1942 Commandos had been used as a spearhead for large-scale amphibious operations in advance of regular units at Madagascar (No. 5 Commando) and at Dieppe (No. 3 and No. 4 Commandos). They were tasked with neutralizing enemy coastal batteries and seizing preliminary objectives, although they were quickly withdrawn following the raids. The Commandos were again used in a similar role in the Mediterranean. During the initial landings in North Africa two units (No. 1 and No. 6 Commando) had been employed in a traditional manner, seizing forts and coastal batteries. The exigencies of the ensuing campaign in Tunisia, however, meant that following the original assault landings a chronic shortage of troops ensued; this meant No. 1 and No. 6 Commandos were retained in the fighting line alongside regular battalions in the British 1st Army for over five months, and 'misused' according to some in a largely conventional role. The limitations in terms of combat effectiveness and administration of the existing unit establishment, intended only for small-scale raiding operations, became apparent all too quickly, both to the Commandos themselves and the staffs of formations to which they had been attached. A lack of supporting weapons, vehicles, administrative personnel and appropriate training cost them dear and limited their employment. While fighting with considerable dash and *élan*, the lightly equipped Commandos proved incapable of carrying out many offensive and defensive operations – defeating enemy counterattacks or capturing defensive positions – with the weapons at their disposal. The reliance placed on surprise, speed, darkness, and meticulous planning to overcome enemy resistance that had characterized earlier raids was insufficient on a conventional field of battle. The administrative side had been disastrous, with Commandos only having those personnel required to despatch the force from the port of embarkation and receive them on their return. Only by using captured vehicles or begging, 'borrowing' or outright theft from other formations could units be maintained in the field for long periods of time, using men withdrawn from the firing line as administrative personnel. Even so, unprecedented demands were placed on surrounding regular units. A high casualty rate was suffered during heavy fighting, moreover, that stretched the existing replacement organization; it was unable to cope under the pressure. Insufficient drafts of trained manpower were received during the campaign resulting in each unit's manpower dwindling; they had to reorganize with the reduced number of troops available. At the beginning of April they had to be withdrawn before the decisive battles took place in Tunisia.

This hard-won experience gained while fighting in North Africa, and planning in progress for the employment of substantial Commando forces during the invasion of Sicily and later Italy, convinced senior officers at the Special Service Brigade's HQ that major changes were needed in its organization and that of individual Commandos. In April 1943 a major reorganization was set in train by Brig Robert Laycock, OC Special Service

Commando order of battle, August/September 1943 (458 all ranks)

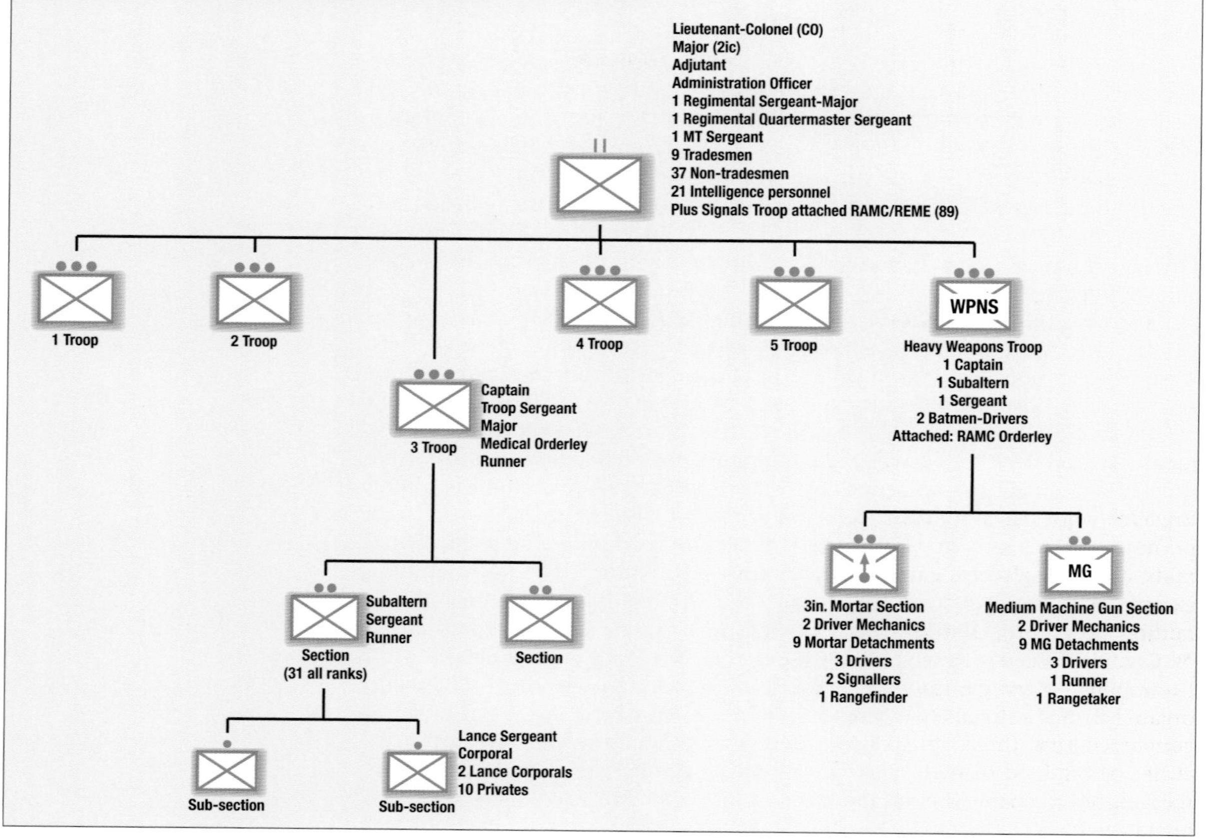
Lieutenant-Colonel (CO)
Major (2ic)
Adjutant
Administration Officer
1 Regimental Sergeant-Major
1 Regimental Quartermaster Sergeant
1 MT Sergeant
9 Tradesmen
37 Non-tradesmen
21 Intelligence personnel
Plus Signals Troop attached RAMC/REME (89)
1 Troop
2 Troop
4 Troop
5 Troop
WPNS
Heavy Weapons Troop
1 Captain
1 Subaltern
1 Sergeant
2 Batmen-Drivers
Attached: RAMC Orderley
3 Troop
Captain
Troop Sergeant
Major
Medical Orderley
Runner
3in. Mortar Section
2 Driver Mechanics
9 Mortar Detachments
3 Drivers
2 Signallers
1 Rangefinder
MG
Medium Machine Gun Section
2 Driver Mechanics
9 MG Detachments
3 Drivers
1 Runner
1 Rangetaker
Subaltern
Sergeant
Runner
Section
(31 all ranks)
Section
Sub-section
Sub-section
Lance Sergeant
Corporal
2 Lance Corporals
10 Privates

Special Service Group order of battle, March 1944

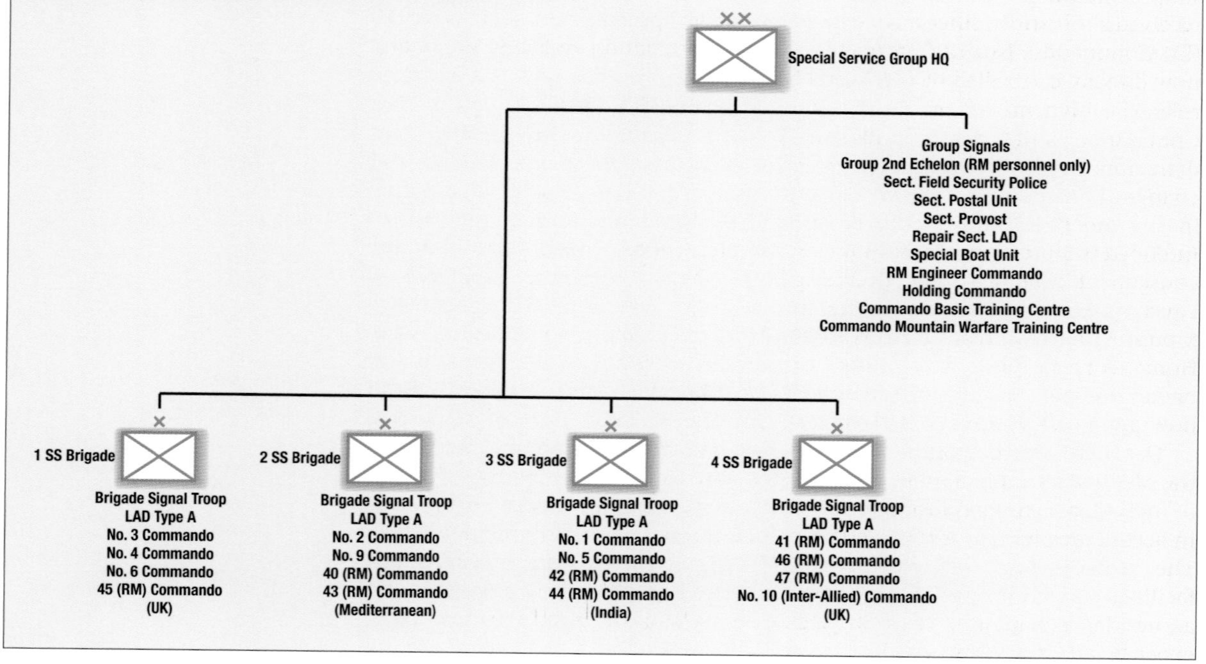
Special Service Group HQ
Group Signals
Group 2nd Echelon (RM personnel only)
Sect. Field Security Police
Sect. Postal Unit
Sect. Provost
Repair Sect. LAD
Special Boat Unit
RM Engineer Commando
Holding Commando
Commando Basic Training Centre
Commando Mountain Warfare Training Centre
1 SS Brigade
Brigade Signal Troop
LAD Type A
No. 3 Commando
No. 4 Commando
No. 6 Commando
45 (RM) Commando
(UK)
2 SS Brigade
Brigade Signal Troop
LAD Type A
No. 2 Commando
No. 9 Commando
40 (RM) Commando
43 (RM) Commando
(Mediterranean)
3 SS Brigade
Brigade Signal Troop
LAD Type A
No. 1 Commando
No. 5 Commando
42 (RM) Commando
44 (RM) Commando
(India)
4 SS Brigade
Brigade Signal Troop
LAD Type A
41 (RM) Commando
46 (RM) Commando
47 (RM) Commando
No. 10 (Inter-Allied) Commando
(UK)

RM Engineer Commando order of battle, 1944

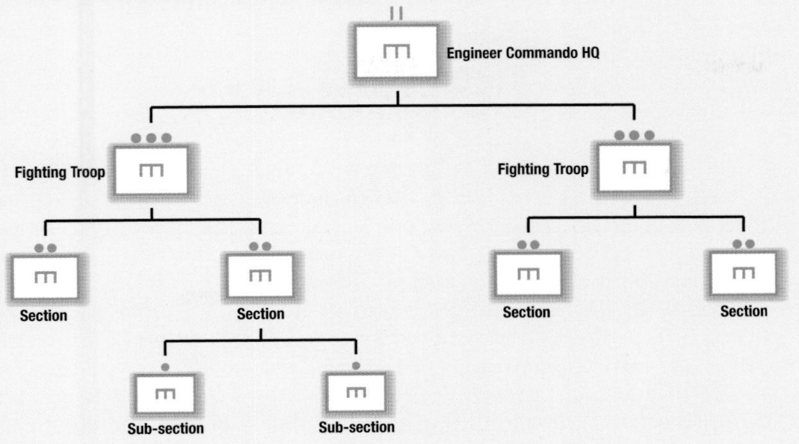
Engineer Commando HQ
Fighting Troop
Fighting Troop
Section
Section
Section
Section
Sub-section
Sub-section

Brigade, who was now fully convinced that in future Commandos would primarily participate in larger-scale operations overseas, mount large-scale raids, and fight alongside regular Army formations in a conventional role to an extent never envisaged before, as well as mounting 'traditional' short-term raiding operations. In a detailed paper submitted to Lord Mountbatten, Chief of Combined Operations, entitled 'Role of the Special Service Brigade and Desirability of Reorganization', he carefully analyzed the existing Commando organization and its likely future employment. The OC Special Service Brigade concluded that three options now existed for the Commandos, who could either be retained in their current form for small-scale raiding, disbanded, or reorganized to enable them 'to take the fullest part in the coming battle' either operating independently or in conjunction with the Field Force. The option of disbandment of the Special Service Brigade and its Commandos was dismissed out of hand. A second option of scaling back the Special Service Brigade and simply retaining the Commandos solely for small-scale raiding operations also received short shrift, since a wide range of smaller special forces, such as No. 10 (IA) Commando, No. 12 Commando, No. 14 Commando and the SSRF (many now directly controlled by SOE), had largely taken over the small-scale raiding role. The high morale, esprit de corps and specialized fighting efficiency of Commando units, which had won the respect of both the enemy and detractors in the UK, meant this option was unacceptable. Instead, major changes in the command structure of the Special Service Brigade and changes in the order of battle of the brigade and of individual Commando units, intended to fit it for use in both the assault phase of an operation and then the consequent extended fighting during the follow up, were recommended by Laycock. These strong recommendations were fully accepted by Lord Louis Mountbatten and in turn the War Office, although the Commander-in-Chief Home Forces still believed the Commandos would not be employed in operations subsequent to the initial amphibious assault. Sicily and Italy, however, quickly proved him wrong.

The increasing employment of the Commando in North-West Europe and the Mediterranean in a more conventional role necessitated the reorganization of individual Commandos, in terms of their organization, arms and equipment in accordance with a new war establishment promulgated in September 1943. The primary aim was to increase both the firepower and administrative facilities of each unit to enable them to carry out their original role and fight alongside regular units for protracted periods of time, although not at the expense of tactical flexibility.

The former was accomplished by adding a heavy weapons troop to the existing six fighting troops in each Commando, incorporating the various weapons (i.e. 3in. mortars and .303 Vickers medium machine guns) that had been employed periodically on an ad-hoc basis by several units, but which had always lacked dedicated officers, crews, or transport vehicles. Each new heavy weapons troop consisted of a mortar section (equipped with two 3in. mortars) and a medium machine gun section (armed with two .303 Vickers guns), with sufficient dedicated personnel to operate them and seven jeeps and trailers to carry them in the field. In addition, the number of Bren LMGs carried by each fighting troop was increased from four to six, making a total of 31 for each Commando (including one held at Commando HQ). A further 12 Bren LMGs were held in reserve at HQ and issued as and when required. Lastly, the number of man-portable 2in. mortars, firing smoke and high-explosive rounds, was increased by one modified parachute mortar (a lighter version of this weapon lacking a base plate and having a shorter barrel) per sub-section, making a total of 36 2in. mortars per Commando, 12 of the ordinary type and 24 modified parachute mortars. Although the latter had a far shorter range than normal, its high rate of fire and flexibility greatly increased the firepower of units.

Each Commando unit was provided with sufficient transport and administrative personnel to make it mobile and self-sufficient at least in the short term in the field. A permanent establishment of vehicles was at last allocated to each unit sufficient for supply, administration and communication purposes in the field. They also facilitated the transport of stores and heavy weapons, and meant approximately two troops and Commando HQ could be transported in its own vehicles. This also gave each Commando a limited mobile reconnaissance capability. A further three motorcycles and two 3-ton trucks were added to the establishment of each Commando, making a total of nine and three respectively. While the CO's car was retained, other cars were replaced by eight far more robust 15cwt trucks capable of carrying heavy loads. Transport for the heavy weapons troop consisted of jeeps and trailers, with a further jeep provided for each troop and Commando HQ.

The heavy prolonged fighting in North Africa had highlighted the inherent weaknesses in the existing system for replacing wastage in Commando units in the field, which clearly required a major overhaul. Following raids, Commando

Men of No. 4 Commando engaged in house to house fighting with German troops at Riva Bella, near Ouistreham, June 1944. Sherman DD tanks of 'B' Squadron, 13/18th Royal Hussars are providing close fire support and cover. (MH 2012)

units had previously remained out of combat for long periods of time, giving them sufficient opportunity to rebuild and absorb new recruits provided in dribs and drabs from the Commando Depot or else transferred from other units. This had been impossible for both Commandos deployed in North Africa, which had suffered heavy losses over a five-month period and had required a substantial draft of trained manpower. Large-scale cross-posting of personnel from other units was no longer judged an acceptable alternative, since it reduced unit efficiency and damaged esprit de corps. A new Operational Holding Commando, based at Wrexham, was formed to address this problem; the downside of this, however, was the disbandment of No. 12 Commando and the RM Holding Commando to find the necessary manpower, given the chronic manpower shortage now affecting the British armed forces as a whole. It enabled a reserve of trained men to be built up until a draft was urgently required to restore to full strength a unit heavily engaged in combat (see *Doctrine and training*).

The lessons learnt by the Commandos during Operation *Torch*, Operation *Husky*, further amphibious landings in Italy, and the ensuing fighting, as well as the detailed planning underway for the long anticipated invasion of North-West Europe, led to the last major changes to the command and control structure and organization of the Special Service Brigade carried out during World War II. A major change in the command structure of the Special Service Brigade had featured in Brig Laycock's proposals, whose responsibility stretched geographically 'from Inverness-shire to the Isle of Wight, and from North Wales to Buckinghamshire' and included 18 subordinate units. This was far greater than normally allocated to a conventional brigade headquarters and imposed a severe strain upon its staff, especially when commanding and controlling simultaneous operations from the different parts of the country. The Special Service Brigade, moreover, was heavily overburdened with dealing with COHQ for policy operations and training; various War Office branches for

A group of NCOs and ORs of No. 48 (Royal Marine) Commando, Holland, March 1945. (A28399)

Y Troop of No. 48 (Royal Marine) Commando boarding an ALC during Operation *Bograt*, Holland, April 1945. (A28403)

administration, discipline and personnel; the individual regional commands in the UK where Commandos were based; and lastly with all operational commands in relation to finding new recruits. Laycock had proposed that henceforward the command of the Special Service Brigade was decentralized by grouping units into three separate brigades (each of three Commandos) each under its own commander, who, in turn, was responsible for his group, thereby freeing Brigade HQ to deal with matters of general policy and large-scale operations. Other various specialized units that had been raised since 1940 were retained under the direct control of its HQ.

The detailed proposals for the enlargement and reorganization of the order of battle of the Special Service Brigade submitted by Brig Robert Laycock in April 1943, involving its division into three Commando groups each of three Commandos and with the remaining specialized units under command of Brigade HQ, were largely overtaken by events. By mid 1943 they were clearly were not far-reaching enough, given a massive increase in the size of the existing Commando organization proposed by the Chiefs of Staff in July 1943 for the projected invasion of France and large-scale amphibious operations in other theatres of war. Extant plans for Operation *Overlord* alone required an increase in the number of available Commandos, with four assigned to each assault division, to carry out such tasks as destroying coastal batteries and protecting the flanks of landing beaches. A new Special Service Group, commanded by Maj Gen Robert Sturges (a highly experienced and very capable Royal Marine), was formed in October 1943. It was tasked with coordinating the various Commando forces following the decision to increase the size of the Commandos by reorganizing and retraining complete units from the redundant Royal Marine Division (which had languished for a considerable period of time in the UK unused) and MNBDOs into new Royal Marine Commandos. This decision was taken to avoid creaming off volunteers from army units, but further reinforced enduring criticism levelled by members of existing Army Commandos that since the new Commandos were not composed of picked volunteers they lacked the same dash, enthusiasm and combat effectiveness of their predecessors. It most certainly did not prove a marriage made in heaven. As Maj Gen James Moulton (who commanded No. 48 (RM) Commando during D-Day and its aftermath) has written:

> Now the Army commandos felt and said that the Marines, unlike themselves, were not volunteers, lacked operational experience and were appropriating themselves prestige they had not won; Marines felt, and usually tried not to say, that while there was much to admire and envy in the well-publicized efforts and records of the Army commandos, not all of it was above criticism and some of it was positively amateurish.[8]

Six new units – Nos. 42–47 (RM) Commandos – were formed with effect from 1 August 1943 on the new unit war establishment, and in turn attended the Commando Depot at Achnacarry. Many men failed to make the grade and were transferred away to other units, partly addressing concerns about maintaining high Commando standards, and other volunteers were brought in. These were not the only additions to the order of battle. With the manpower demands of Operation *Overlord* (the invasion of Normandy) steadily increasing, a further Royal Marine Commando – No. 48 (Royal Marine) Commando – joined the Special Service Group in March 1944, with its officers and men rushed through a truncated course at Achnacarry.

Table 4: origins of Royal Marine Commando units

1 RM Battalion	No. 42 (RM) Commando
2 RM Battalion	No. 43 (RM) Commando
3 RM Battalion	No. 44 (RM) Commando
5 RM Battalion	No. 45 (RM) Commando
9 RM Battalion	No. 46 (RM) Commando
10 RM Battalion	No. 47 (RM) Commando
7 RM Battalion	No. 48 (RM) Commando (formed March 1944)

The new Special Service Group HQ – effectively in charge of a large division, although one lacking supporting arms and services – took command of four newly formed Special Service brigades, each consisting of four Commandos under the overall command of a brigadier. Although it was originally intended to form separate Army and Royal Marine Commando Brigades, this idea was nipped in the bud for fear of sparking divisive inter-service rivalry and to capitalize on a proven track record of mixed formations fighting in the Mediterranean theatre of war. Instead, mixed Special Service brigades (1–4), consisting of both Army and Royal Marine units, were organized. Two brigades remained in North-West Europe, while another served in the Mediterranean and a fourth was despatched to South-East Asia Command. Several smaller units were also formed. In August 1943 a new Royal Marine Engineer Commando company was raised at Dorchester in response to Laycock's earlier recommendation for such a unit to make the Special Service Brigade self-sufficient. It was expanded to form a complete Commando of three troops, one of which was later sent with 3rd Special Service Brigade to India.

The order of battle of the Army and Royal Marine Commandos and that of individual units remained largely unchanged for the rest of World War II. The new Special Service Group organization worked well, with the four new subordinate Special Service Brigade HQs heavily committed to battle for the rest of the war, spearheading major amphibious operations or else fighting alongside regular units as assault or light infantry. Some small-scale raiding operations continued, most notably along the eastern seaboard of the Adriatic, where elements of 2nd Commando Brigade fought alongside Yugoslav partisans on offshore islands and along the coast. A heavy strain was imposed on the replacement system, however, by heavy losses suffered by the Commandos. Between 6 June and 30 September 1944, 39 officers and 371 ORs were killed, 114 officers and 1,324 ORs were wounded, and 7 officers and 162 ORs were reported missing. As Messenger has noted, this represented approximately 50 percent of the total war establishment. Due to a combination of the high standard demanded by the Commandos and the number of acceptable volunteers from training establishments and the Field Army dwindling, the replacement organization struggled to keep up with wastage on occasion. Only a few minor changes occurred in the order of battle. On 30 June 1944, No. 2 SBS was disbanded, since they were largely surplus to requirements following the invasion of North-West Europe. On 6 December 1944 the hated title 'Special Service', with its associations with the German SS, was finally abandoned with Commando being substituted and applied to all formations. The Special Service Group became the Commando Group while Special Service Brigades became Commando Brigades, under which name they fought until the end of World War II. Further changes in the war establishment of Commando units, however, were in train for the prosecution of the war against Japan. Indeed, a new Commando (Light) organization had been agreed for units being despatched to the Far East in the autumn of 1945. It involved the addition of further 3in. mortars to each heavy weapons troop and far greater administrative personnel, given the distances between bases and operational areas in theatre. The dropping of atomic bombs on Hiroshima and Nagasaki and the sudden ending of World War II meant these changes were never implemented.

The GOC 8th Army chats to Lt Col John Durnford-Slater following the attack on Termoli in Italy, 19 October 1943. (E26179)

Doctrine and training

The highly specialized combat mission initially assigned to Commando units, mounting small-scale offensive raiding operations of very short duration, posed responsible officers great practical problems in terms of doctrine and developing appropriate training. Although studied in staff colleges, only lip service had been paid to carrying out amphibious operations in the UK before World War II and as a result no training manuals existed whatsoever upon which Commando training could be based. The tactical 'bible' of the British Army – Field Service Regulations – and the training manuals of the different arms were completely silent on the subject. Given this dearth of relevant experience, training manuals, and appropriate specialized training regimes, much had to be learnt in a very short space of time. Indeed, new fighting methods, skills, drills, and techniques had to be hurriedly devised as they went along to fit the volunteers and the changing organization of Commandos/ Special Service battalions for their new fighting role, and to build up physical fitness and endurance. This 'emerging doctrine' fortunately built upon a solid bedrock of basic training already given to their men, and drew upon the same basic doctrine employed by the rest of the British Army, as laid down in a series of Military Training Pamphlets issued during the war years.

The COs of newly formed Commandos in both the Middle East and UK played a key role in devising an appropriate doctrine for their men. Indeed, training was initiated by and the immediate responsibility of unit COs, being very loosely supervised by senior formation commanders, allowing them considerable latitude in method from unit to unit. Progress was hampered, moreover, by chronic shortages of arms, equipment and weapons. Fortunately officers with the necessary initiative, drive, determination, and skills were found within Commando ranks, who were left to their own devices to develop fighting methods and appropriate training methods to be imparted to their

French Commandos practise making an opposed landing at Achnacarry. (H31408)

units. Doctrine was initially directed towards small-scale raiding operations, with men trained to fight as individuals or in very small groups. The tentative training regime – quickly acknowledged as the toughest in the UK – developed by individual Commandos was intended to produce a self-reliant, all-round, first-class, essentially light infantry soldier, possessing both high morale and offensive spirit and capable of carrying out daring, highly aggressive raids. As the CO of No. 2 Commando directed:

> The object of Special Service is to have available a fully trained body of first class soldiers ready for active offensive operations against an enemy in any part of the world. Irregular warfare demands the highest standards of initiative, mental alertness and physical fitness, together with the maximum skill at arms. No Commando can feel confident of success unless all ranks are capable of thinking for themselves; of thinking quickly.[9]

Fortunately the volunteers who flocked to Commando ranks were normally highly motivated men of a high standard already: the threat of being ignominiously 'RTUed' permanently hung over the heads of all ranks, and ensured training standards, military efficiency, and discipline were always high. The imminent threat of German invasion, moreover, and the widespread desire to strike back against the enemy added considerable incentive to train hard.

Senior Commando officers were not left completely to their own devices. The War Office was not idle and eventually issued its own guidelines to Commandos, since the overall direction of their training remained a responsibility of the Director of Military Training. *Commando Training Instruction No. 1* dated 1 August 1940 was intended to prepare Commandos for short duration 'smash and grab raids into enemy territory' not lasting more than 24 hours and carried out by a force no larger than a single Commando unit. It directed:

A French Commando armed with a Thompson SMG training in Scotland. (H31424)

> The creation of such a force calls for the highest standard of training, personal and collective discipline, courage, skill, determination and imagination in all ranks – backed up by the inspired leadership and organizing ability on the part of their commanders.[10]

To accomplish this objective, training aimed to produce highly developed team spirit and esprit de corps, and on the part of the individual considerable self-reliance and resourcefulness. Following its formation, the HQ of the Special Service Brigade also produced a series of training guidelines for its subordinate units as the war progressed, intended to fit its units for their highly specialized and changing role.

The training given to all Commandos throughout the rest of World War II placed considerable emphasis on developing offensive spirit, mental and physical fitness, and self-reliance. An extremely tough training regimen always followed, emphasizing the importance of high levels of physical fitness, instilled by speed marches, long endurance marches over difficult terrain carrying full arms and equipment, and swimming – again wearing full equipment. As noted, a high degree of self-reliance was always regarded as a key element of Commando instruction. In part, it was engendered by billeting troops amongst the local population and making them responsible for their own food with a generous messing allowance, and for turning up as and when required for military duty. Each soldier looked after his own weapons and equipment and had to display initiative under all circumstances, sharply contrasting with the mainstream British Army of the time. It also relieved them from irksome domestic duties required in barracks and freed them for training. Even so, the importance of strict discipline was not overlooked. As the CO of 2 Commando observed in his 'Commando Catechism': 'At all times a high standard of discipline is essential, and the constant desire by all ranks to be fitter and better trained than anyone else.'[11]

The Commando training regimen demanded an extremely high standard of basic military skills, covering skill-at-arms, marksmanship, and field craft, with all ranks capable of foraging for food and living in the field for lengthy periods of time without relying on normal supply lines. All ranks were expected to be marksmen and to employ all the different types of weapons issued to each Commando with skill, as well as mastering innovative new methods of weapon handling developed by these elite units. Training also included instruction on various types of captured German and Italian weapons. Unarmed combat always formed an important part of instruction along with hand-to-hand combat, using the distinctive Fairbairn-Sykes fighting knife and other types of knives developed for the Special Service Brigade. Under the expert guidance of Maj William Fairbairn and Eric Sykes, former Shanghai policemen, a high level of efficiency was achieved and offensive spirit inculcated. Night operations were judged vital for success, with emphasis placed on the use of map and compass and stealth. Although units had few vehicles actually on establishment, all ranks were trained to drive different types of cars, lorries, and motorcycles. New skills outside the normal run of military training had to be developed from scratch. Cliff climbing, mountaineering, watermanship and boat work using landing craft and small boats always formed an essential element of instruction, since they always formed a key part of amphibious operations carried out by the Special Service Brigade. Such cliff assault skills meant Commandos could avoid obvious landing places and go ashore on rocky headlands. Handling explosives and elementary demolition work and sabotage were normal, using different types of high explosive. Initially, parachuting also featured as part of the Commando regime for No. 1 and No. 2 Commandos, but eventually No. 2 Commando became No. 11 Special Air Service Battalion and then 1st Battalion Parachute Regiment, and left the Special Service Brigade.

The newly formed Commandos drew upon a range of existing GHQ home forces and other schools for specialized knowledge about such subjects as intelligence work and signalling to fit them for their new role. The Commandos benefited in particular during the early war years from tuition at the Irregular Warfare School (later dubbed the Special Training Centre, or STC), established in May 1940 in the mountains and glens of Scotland at Inverailort Castle, Lochailort (seven miles from Fort William), by David Stirling. Initially, Lord Lovat, Michael Calvert, and Spencer Chapman were amongst its distinguished instructors. Originally set up specifically to train 'special forces', it played a key role from July 1940 onwards in training small batches of Commando officers, NCOs, and ORs during a series of short courses teaching the more specialized skills required for their new role. Michael Calvert, for example, taught demolition work, while unarmed combat was the province of Fairbairn and Sykes, who taught as an added dimension their personal philosophy on personal aggression, which in the longer term had considerable influence on the Commandos. Taught amidst the mountains and lochs of Scotland, the school's syllabus included field craft, demolition work, close-quarter combat, weapon training, and signals, as well as including endurance marches, cliff climbing, swimming with full kit, seamanship and boat work, night operations, map reading, and stalking. From March 1941 onwards two Commando fighting troops were sent in turn for special instruction, eventually involving the attendance of all men from early Commandos. Each course culminated in a three-day test of endurance. As one student recalled:

> The impact on us of this specialist training and of these feats of endurance was extraordinary. Even the humblest and smallest solider quickly developed into a man 'twice his height', as it were, who thought nothing of the hardships which would have been impossible to him and his mates a few weeks before arriving in that lonely part of Scotland.[12]

With the demand for replacements increasing, the STC also began training recruits for the Special Service Brigade, before onward despatch to their new units. A small holding section was established at the nearby Achnacarry Castle, where trained recruits were held pending transfer to operational units. By early 1942 the STC had become largely surplus to requirements, however, since the many Special Forces forming part of the British order of battle were highly trained and possessed considerable experience, and it was converted into a naval training centre.

Achnacarry – the Commando Depot

The ad-hoc system developed during the early war years for selecting new recruits, and the long-term development of Commando doctrine and training, generally served individual units well in preparing them for raiding operations. It was not, however, without its faults. Little thought initially was given to defensive operations, for example, since the precise combat mission assigned to Commando units did not acknowledge them and the organization, light scales of weapons equipment, and training was unsuited to them. On occasion this serious gap in military knowledge and military training caused serious tactical difficulties, especially towards the end of the war when Commando units fought in a conventional role. The training carried out was initially handicapped by chronic shortages of necessary equipment and weapons. Hard-won lessons gained on active service were gradually assimilated into in-house training instructions and letters produced within the Special Service Brigade. A downside of leaving training as the primary responsibility of unit COs, however, was a marked variation in method and standards of instruction, as well as difficulty in passing on lessons learnt by experienced Commandos to other units.

Commando Basic Training Centre, Achnacarry, outline order of battle

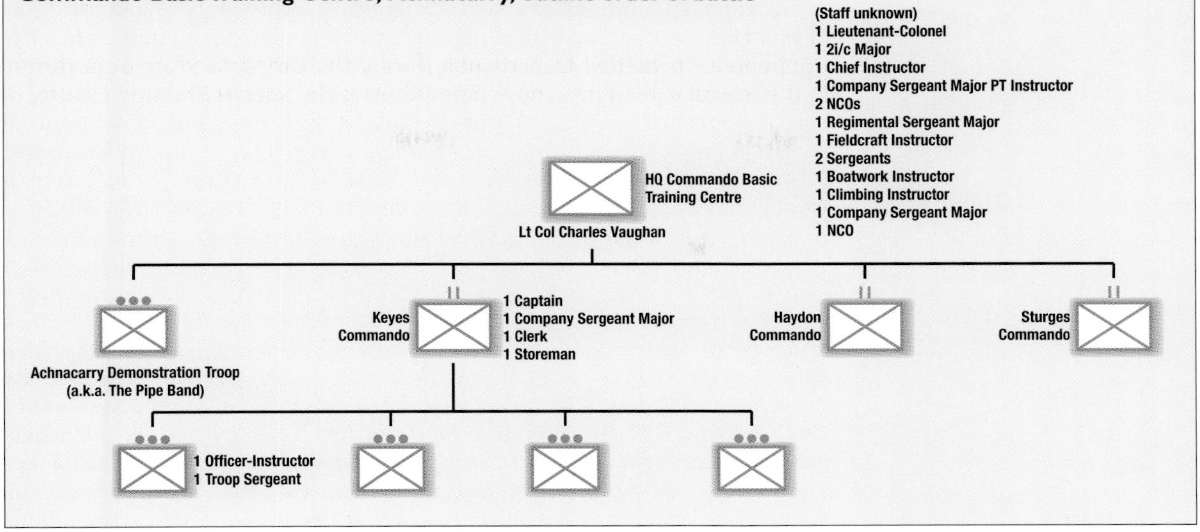
(Staff unknown)
1 Lieutenant-Colonel
1 2i/c Major
1 Chief Instructor
1 Company Sergeant Major PT Instructor
2 NCOs
1 Regimental Sergeant Major
1 Fieldcraft Instructor
2 Sergeants
1 Boatwork Instructor
1 Climbing Instructor
1 Company Sergeant Major
1 NCO
HQ Commando Basic Training Centre
Lt Col Charles Vaughan
Achnacarry Demonstration Troop (a.k.a. The Pipe Band)
Keyes Commando
1 Captain
1 Company Sergeant Major
1 Clerk
1 Storeman
Haydon Commando
Sturges Commando
1 Officer-Instructor
1 Troop Sergeant

To put Commando training on a more formal standing, Brig Charles Haydon established a Commando Depot in February 1942 (later renamed the Commando Basic Training Centre). It was intended to meet the demand for complete new units and also the constant demands for replacements to fill gaps in existing Commandos. Occupying the remote country house and estate at Achnacarry in West Scotland (home of Sir Donald Cameron, the Chief of Clan Cameron of Lochiel), this new training establishment was located 14 miles from Fort William. Under the command of Maj (later Col) Charles Vaughan, 'Castle Commando' quickly earned a fearsome reputation, henceforward being made responsible for training complete new units, sub-units and individual replacements with only a few exceptions.

The training regime developed at Achnacarry went a long way to addressing the problems with doctrine identified by Brig Charles Haydon, developing training regimens, and providing an adequate flow of recruits. The innovative and physically demanding course devised by the highly experienced former 2i/c

Operational Holding Commando order of battle, 1944

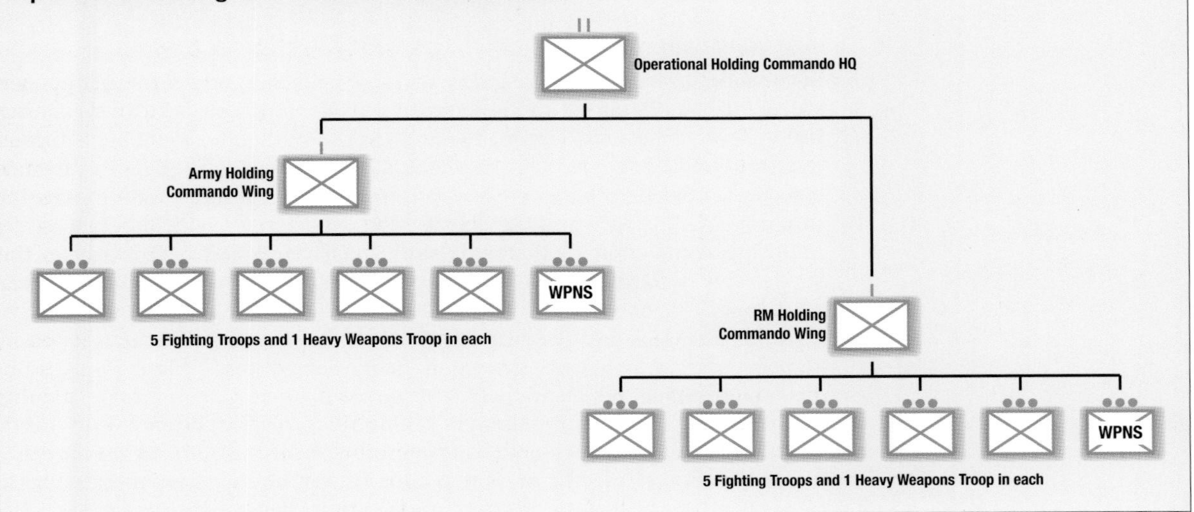
Operational Holding Commando HQ
Army Holding Commando Wing
WPNS
5 Fighting Troops and 1 Heavy Weapons Troop in each
RM Holding Commando Wing
WPNS
5 Fighting Troops and 1 Heavy Weapons Troop in each

of No. 4 Commando (a veteran of Word War I and a former RSM in the Guards and Buffs), was far in advance of anything being employed by the British Army at the time and produced high-quality recruits. The high standards demanded by this striking, upright, but rather portly soldier helped shape the Commandos for the rest of the war. As one former instructor has recalled:

> [Vaughan] accepted nothing but the best, whether it be fitness, weapon training and musketry, fieldcraft and tactics, drill and turnout, or even in the more apparently mundane matters of administration which included feeding and hygiene. Together all these factors made the 'whole' – and the self-disciplined and reliant Commando soldier, 'fit to fight and fighting fit', with high morale, willing and capable of tackling any military task, under any circumstances and against any odds.[13]

Achnacarry was designed to test the physical fitness and the mental resilience of the officers, NCOs, and men that passed through its gates. With a handpicked staff, all capable of outperforming their students, carefully devised and highly realistic exercises were run, all with a generous allocation of live ammunition and explosives, for both officers and men. From the outset it tested the endurance of each intake, with a forced eight-mile march for new students, carrying full kit, from Spean Bridge Railway Station ending with a march past a row of 'graves' of men who had died from failure to observe elementary military precautions. Following a rousing introductory speech setting out the course, Vaughan pulled no punches in outlining the difficulties faced by students and observed many men present would be 'RTUed'. A series of gruelling speed marches carrying full arms and equipment up and down nearby mountains, endurance marches, arduous assault courses including a death slide over the River Arkeig and a so-called 'Tarzan' course were carried out by each intake. River crossing, rock climbing, night marching, and other strenuous activities filled each day and many nights. Nearby Ben Nevis was a final challenge presented to students. Cross-country runs and physical training, including boxing matches, helped bring trainees to a peak of military fitness. Spartan living conditions and limited food cooked by themselves in Nissen huts or under canvas in bell tents, provided only the barest comforts. Even so the strictest attention was paid to smartness and turnout, with men left to clean uniforms, buff boots and polish brass despite coming in soaked and covered in mud from each day's training. Square bashing was a regular feature, and throughout the course saluting was mandatory, with the Commandant insisting it provided a solid foundation for developing self-discipline.

The course at the Commando Basic Training Centre covered in addition all the key elements of Commando training previously carried out at unit level: close-order drill, physical training, unarmed combat, advanced weapon training, bayonet drill, assault courses, speed marching, field craft, map reading, and night patrolling. Boat handling and watermanship were taught on nearby Loch Lochy, using assorted whalers, cutters, landing craft, dories, canoes, rubber dinghies, rafts, and folding canvas boats; the Loch had many locations along its shoreline suitable for dry-shod and wet-shod landings. Swimming was also of particular importance. The demanding course was progressive, with troop training following completion of the initial individual stage, and each stage leading successively onto the next. As one Royal Marine student later described:

> In the first week the men were dead beat physically, morale was at its lowest point and many felt like giving up. In the second week things started to come together and the trainees were not so ready to give up. By the third week the physical exertions were beginning to pay off, morale was good and all thoughts of giving up had been erased from their minds. The fourth week saw the trainees in superb physical condition, their morale was excellent, every man experienced a high sense of accomplishment.[14]

Lt Gen T.L. Hunton and Lt Col Charles Vaughan watch No. 43 (Royal Marine) Commando undergoing training at Achnacarry. (H32667)

Throughout each course, officers of all ranks, ordered to leave batmen behind, were expected to outperform their men in all respects during intensive training carried out by fully armed and heavily equipped troops. Each course culminated with a simulated 'opposed' night landing during which live ammunition was freely expended to add realism. Many men failed to make the grade on each course and were ruthlessly 'RTUed', while a concomitant of using live ammunition and explosives was a 'butcher's bill' of dead and wounded.

The Commando Basic Training Centre ably fulfilled its brief of standardizing training and all ensuring a high standard of recruits, sub-units and later complete new units in specialized Commando skills. It earned a fearsome reputation for toughness. Indeed, the tough, relentless and physically demanding course devised and implemented at Achnacarry was unique for the time in many ways, in large part due to its innovative CO. Dubbed the 'Laird of Achnacarry', 'The Rommel of the North', 'Earl of Spean', 'Lord Fort William' and the 'Wolf of Badenoch' amongst other titles, the highly respected Vaughan made a decisive contribution to Commando training. As one officer described:

> I think it is no exaggeration to say that the commandos owe as much to him and his hard work, vision and amazing enthusiasm, as to any other person. He is one of the greatest characters of the commandos, and the stories about him and his depot are legion.

Similarly, Louis Mountbatten later wrote:

> The right site had to be found and the right man. Achnacarry could hardly have been bettered for the site, and Charles Vaughan could certainly not have been bettered as the man.[15]

It was certainly an unforgettable experience for its students, who lived perpetually soaked to the skin amongst the seemingly permanent rain of Scotland. Many foreign nationals also passed through its gates, beginning with the Free French 1st Marine Company who attended Achnacarry in March 1942. They were followed in June 1942 by members of the newly raised US 1st Ranger Battalion, commanded by Major William Darby, whose officers and men learnt

Commandos crossing a river on a 'toggle bridge' under simulated artillery fire, at the Commando Training Depot at Achnacarry, Invernessshire, Scotland, January 1943. (H 26620)

much about Commando tactics and techniques that stood them in good stead for the rest of the war. Between its opening and the end of the war approximately 25,000 men passed through Achnacarry's doors, including Americans, Belgians, Dutchmen, Frenchmen, Norwegians, Poles, and British servicemen from Royal Navy Beachhead Commandos and RAF Servicing Commandos.

The output of highly trained Commando officers, NCOs and ORs from the Commando Basic Training Centre, however, was not always sufficient to meet demand by early 1943, as the intensity of military operations in North Africa involving units of the Special Service Brigade increased. Late in 1943 a small Operational Holding Commando became part of the order of battle of the Special Service Brigade. It had a dual role. Henceforward it received all volunteers for the Special Service Brigade, and before onward despatch to the CBTC ensured they were physically fit, ready in all respects for individual training, and were all first-class shots. Following completion of basic training at the CBTC at Achnacarry, fully trained Commando soldiers were then transferred back to the Operational Holding Commando, where they received advanced collective and combined training and a high standard of physical fitness was maintained until such time as a unit in the field required a draft.

The Commando Basic Training Centre was not the only specialized training establishment set up and used specifically by the Commandos during World War II. Another smaller unit was set up to train Commandos for operations in snow-covered mountains, cliff assaults, landings on rocky shores, and handling small craft and canoes during coastal raids. To give students instruction in operating in cold, inhospitable terrain a Commando Mountain and Snow Warfare Training Camp opened at Braemar in Aberdeenshire in Scotland on 1 December 1942, in response to growing pressure to carry out operations in the inhospitable mountains of Norway. Under the command of RAF Squadron Leader Frank Smythe, a world-famous Everest mountaineer, and with Maj John Hunt (later the conqueror of Mount Everest) as Chief Instructor, this new training establishment taught troops how to live, move on foot and on skis, and fight in inhospitable, snowy conditions. It proved a successful double act. As Hunt later recalled in his memoirs:

> Frank and I got on well together ... we made an excellent partnership. He was a gentle, most unwarlike character, whose main contribution to the work at the Centre was to impart a deep, poetic love of the mountains to

> the tough, high-spirited wearers of the Green Beret. His achievements won him respect, the more so because of his slight physique. I was able to supply the element of military pragmatism to the exercises, which tended to be rather aimless mountain walks which Frank enjoyed so much.[16]

Its first students were those in North Force drawn from various different Commandos, including men from No. 12 Commando, No. 10 (IA) Commando, and No. 14 Commando. They were followed in turn by No. 1 and No. 4 Commandos. Amidst the Cairngorn mountains surrounding Braemar, a six-week course covered moving over difficult ground on foot and on skis, dealing with poor weather conditions and living, moving and fighting amidst intense cold, knowledge of Arctic rations and mountain equipment, and navigation under poor weather conditions. In 1943 it moved to Llanwrst in North Wales where, as the renamed Commando Mountain Warfare Training Camp, under the command of Geoffrey Rees-Jones, it concentrated on mountain warfare, rock climbing, and mountaineering in general. A final move took place in December 1943 to St Ives in Cornwall where this small training establishment gave instruction in cliff assaults and landings on rocky shorelines to three Royal Marine Commandos as part of their preparations for D-Day.

Training from late 1943 to the end of the war

The training regimen taught by the staff at Achnacarry and by the Commando units undergoing refresher training or serving at the 'sharp end' underwent constant development during the course of the war, as the organization of units developed, new arms and equipment were issued, and fresh techniques suited to their specialized role were developed, including the use of specialized landing craft and other assault equipment. A common training regimen was followed by both the Army and Royal Marine Commandos following the creation of the Special Service Group, with the new GOC Special Service Group determined to ensure the maintenance of high standards by both services. As Sturges directed in October 1943:

> Commandos, due to their past distinguished efforts in various theatres of war, have now won a war reputation with other Services that is second to none. In spite of this enviable position neither individuals nor units can ever afford to sit back and live on this reputation and newly won traditions but go, and keep 'all out', to live up to their well and hardly won record of distinction.[17]

Even so, to ensure the new Royal Marine Commandos were operational as soon as possible the syllabus of Achnacarry was slightly simplified in late 1943. A shortened course, moreover, was run for the last Commando raised – No. 48 (RM) Commando – since it was needed in haste for the Normandy landings. The changing combat mission of the Commandos from 1943 led to some changes in the thrust of instruction away from solely raiding operations to a more conventional light infantry role, with considerably heavier fire support on call from the artillery and tactical air power. Before Operation *Overlord*, for example, training for both Army and Marine Commandos widened to include operations by two or more Commandos working together to seize set objectives, and cooperation with regular units and formations during the follow-up phase of major amphibious landings, including armoured and artillery units. It did not, however, lead to the complete abandonment of normal Commando instruction that stood units, for example those serving in the Adriatic, in good stead until the end of the war.

Tactics

The minor tactics, general fighting methods and various techniques employed by the Commandos during early raids and harassing attacks were highly specialized, with these predicated initially on making surprise 'smash and grab,' 'butcher or bolt,' 'tip and run' or more simply 'hit and run' small-scale raids within close striking distance of the coast. None would last longer than 24 hours before the raiding force withdrew to a secure base in the UK. In practice, these specialized elite troops always employed irregular fighting methods, as opposed to conventional tactics employed by regular army units who were normally dependent upon fighting set-piece battles and upon massing superior firepower from the supporting arms and services. Commando fighting methods always stressed the offensive at all times, with the organization of Commando raiding forces deliberately kept as loose as possible. All operations normally took place at night, with the hours of darkness employed to cover the seaborne approach, amphibious landings, the attack itself upon the chosen objective, and finally the withdrawal back to waiting landing craft. Raids were always heavily dependent throughout on surprise, stealth, and speed for success, as well as careful intelligence gathering, meticulous planning and the rehearsal of specific tasks before each mission began. A considerable effort was placed on deception, 'cunning', and an indirect approach to avoid contact and a pitched battle with organized bodies of enemy troops, who were normally far greater in number and more heavily armed than a raiding party. Indeed, the primary aim of most Commando raids was to strike quickly and with decisive effect and then get away before being brought to action. This was vital since the Commandos simply lacked the heavy support weapons – medium machine guns, mortars, armour, or artillery of any sort – to mount a concerted attack on an alerted, well-defended position occupied by heavily armed conventional troops. Instead, deficiencies in

Men of No. 4 (Army) Commando, 1st Special Service Brigade, marching from their assembly camp to Southampton for embarkation to Normandy, early June 1944. (BU1178)

armament and supporting fire had to be counter-balanced by individualism and by surprise, mobility, and devastating shock effect created by using automatic weapons and grenades at close quarters to overcome enemy resistance. The Commandos normally sought to exploit enemy weaknesses by attacking where least expected. This was achieved by virtue of highly specialized training and by landing at places such as rocky shorelines or at the foot of precipitous cliffs, judged impassable to conventional troops. Infiltration in and around enemy defences always played a key role with a *coup de main* often employed to seize key points before the enemy was alerted. Such attacks were always made with considerable speed and violence before withdrawing with equal rapidity back to base. Fire and movement and simple battle drills were always key elements of Commando fighting methods based on the light weapons at each unit's disposal, with the only source of heavy fire support during opposed operations normally originating from warships lying close off-shore, or from the air. The nature of raiding operations meant the Commandos gave very little thought to defensive tactics during the early war years, since all operations were intended to be only of short duration and with units withdrawing aboard ship after their initial object had been achieved.

Following their 1943 reorganization and re-equipment, the Commandos increasingly employed more conventional tactics, primarily acting as assault or light infantry. No longer could surprise form the basis for a plan of attack or darkness be relied on alone to cover the approach and withdrawal from an objective. The Commandos still always employed highly aggressive light infantry fighting methods, in which fire and manoeuvre and battle drills played a key role, during both the initial amphibious assault and ensuing conventional operations ashore pitted against regular, alerted enemy troops. A crucial difference that enabled these comparatively small and lightly equipped elite units to take their place on a conventional battlefield, however, was the reorganization and re-equipment of each unit with heavy infantry-support weapons – .303 Vickers medium machine guns and 3in. mortars – giving them their own source of badly needed direct and indirect firepower. The addition of the necessary vehicles for tactical transportation and supply and administrative personnel, moreover, gave them both tactical mobility and allowed them to remain in the field for protracted periods of time, unlike before. The possession

Commandos of 1st Special Service Brigade land from an LCI(S) on 'Queen Red' Beach at La Breche, at approximately 0840 hours, 6 June 1944. (B5103)

Men of 4th Special Service Brigade's HQ make their way from LCI(S)s onto 'Nan Red' Beach, Juno Area, at St Aubin-sur-Mer at about 0900 hours on 6 June 1944. (B5218)

of such heavy weapons by each Commando, as well as the high proportion of automatic weapons and light mortars in each fighting troop compared to an ordinary unit of the same size, enabled these numerically small units to mount concerted attacks for the first time, operating alone or alongside other units, on a well-defended position occupied by conventional troops. They also enabled effective resistance to determined enemy attacks when on the defensive. A combination of growing skill, training, and experience meant Commandos were capable of and increasingly employed combined arms tactics (working in close cooperation with tanks, artillery and tactical air power), greatly increasing overall combat effectiveness. This was all the more important since overall they essentially remained smaller and lightly equipped compared to other infantry battalions and remained heavily dependent on fire support from other supporting arms, especially when engaged in pitched battles. The high morale, training, and expertise of Commando units and their specialized organization and equipment, however, were still reflected in many fighting methods employed. To dominate the battlefield, Commando tactics always exploited Commando skills: the offensive always remained a key element, with naked aggression encouraged amongst all ranks. A combination of aggressive patrolling, ambushes, and infiltration in advance of the forward edge of the battle area helped redress the balance between themselves and more heavily armed, conventional enemy units. Night operations still played a key part, with troops lying up by day and striking at vulnerable points behind enemy lines. Small-scale landings to outflank the enemy deep behind enemy lines were also employed in some theatres of war, aimed at demolishing bridges, blocking enemy lines of communication, and spreading alarm and confusion.

Commando uniform, equipment and weapons

The Commandos were largely indistinguishable from the rest of the British Army when formed in 1940, wearing standard British battledress uniform, 37-pattern webbing and equipment. Initially, the headdress and insignia of the parent units from which Commando volunteers originated were retained and worn. Some units quickly adopted distinctive headdress of their own. No. 2 Commando adopted Scottish headdress for all ranks, while No. 11 (Scottish) Commando proudly wore the Tam O'Shanter with a back hackle support behind the badge of the wearer's home regiment. Distinctive new shoulder titles, lanyards and sleeve badges, and in some cases Troop patches designed by the men were quickly added to mark their prestigious new role. This individuality enjoyed by Commando units did not last long. A degree of standardization was started with the introduction of the distinctive Green Beret, common unit titles and the distinctive Combined Operations badge from 1942 (replaced by a Special Service Group sleeve badge in 1945) for both Army and Royal Marine Commandos.

As the war progressed the Commandos' uniforms and equipment gradually evolved to fit them for their raiding and essentially light infantry role. Superfluous equipment was simply left behind (such as large, cumbersome and heavy packs and anti-gas protective equipment), and heavy and bulky steel helmets replaced by practical woolly cap comforters. Lightweight rubber-soled gym shoes that facilitated silent movement replaced heavy ammunition boots on operations. To ensure a degree of safety during landing operations inflatable lifebelts were normally worn and toggle ropes, capable of being linked together to form long ropes, were issued to assist in scaling cliffs and overcoming obstacles. The Commandos were the first to employ Bergen rucksacks to carry heavy loads of ammunition, explosives, fuses and demolition stores. Fitted with a range of straps, the Bergen could carry an extremely heavy load. A battle jerkin or assault jerkin was produced in 1942 to alleviate discomfort caused wearing this item over normal battle dress. Later during the war the airborne force's loose-fitting distinctive camouflage Denison smocks became standard issue on operations.

The Army Commandos and later Royal Marine Commandos always carried an extremely light scale of personal arms, as befitted their role as light or assault infantry. Throughout the war the Commandos largely employed British standard infantry weapons, including bolt-action .303 Short Magazine Lee-Enfield rifles with long sword bayonets (replaced by the No. 4 version with spike bayonet later in the war), .45in. Thompson sub-machine guns, and the superb bipod-mounted .303 Bren light machine gun. Initially, the .38 revolver formed the only sidearm issued to the Commandos, but US Colt .45in.-calibre automatic pistols, with a seven-round magazine, quickly replaced these. A range of edged weapons and clubs equipped them for hand-to-hand close-quarter combat and 'silent killing' upon which the Commandos always placed considerable emphasis. In particular, various models of the distinctive Fairbairn-Sykes fighting knife were carried by the UK-based Commandos, while the Middle East Commandos had their own distinctive Fanny – a combined knife and knuckleduster.

The tried and tested venerable Short Magazine Lee-Enfield (SMLE) Rifle Mk III, originally introduced into British service in 1907, remained standard issue for the Commandos during the early war years. With an effective range of up 3,000 yards, this highly accurate, rugged and extremely reliable weapon was probably the finest manually operated bolt-action rifle in the world. With a

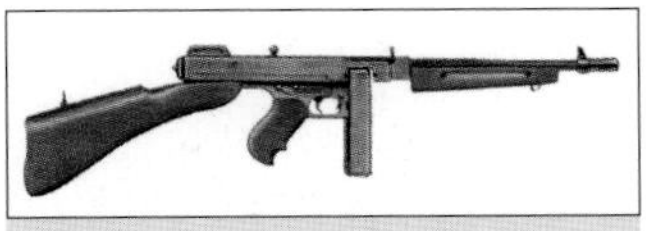

The Thompson sub machine gun
The .45in.-calibre Thompson sub machine gun became the iconic weapon employed by the British Commandos during World War II. Large numbers of these 'Tommy-guns' – weighing in at 10½lb. – were brought from the US during the early war years. Initially they were equipped with drum magazines, holding 50 rounds, but the Commandos soon discarded these and relied instead on 20-round box magazines, given their greater reliability (lack of jamming) and the ease with which extra magazines could be carried on active service. With a cyclic rate of fire of 675 rounds per minute, the Thompson was capable of delivering short bursts of devastating short-range fire that had great shock effect.

The Vickers machine gun
This was the standard medium machine gun used throughout the British and other Commonwealth armies during World War II. It provided a fast, flexible source of fire support to Commando units and was capable of firing 60 shots per minute (rated as slow fire) and 250 as rapid fire. The water-cooled Vickers was accurate up to 1,100 yards but could reach much farther using both direct and indirect fire against a target. The weapon was fired by grasping both traversing handles and depressing the trigger with both thumbs, and was fully automatic as long as the trigger was depressed or until it ran out of ammunition.

The PIAT

The Projector Infantry Anti-Tank (PIAT) was the replacement for the unpopular Boyes 0.5in. anti-tank rifle and came into Commando service early in 1943. This simple and crudely constructed weapon consisted of a cylindrical steel tube, housing a powerful steel spring, at the end of which was a spigot and crude trough into which an HE projectile was placed. The shaped-charge round it fired proved extremely effective at short range (up to 100 yards) and more than a match for the armour on most German tanks. Unlike the US bazooka or German *panzerfaust* it produced no back blast when fired, enabling it be used from within confined spaces. Unfortunately it was unwieldy to carry and also extremely heavy, weighing in at 31.7 lb with each projectile at 3 lb. The spring that fired the projectile, moreover, had a 90kg draw and required considerable strength and skill. By the end of the war some 115,000 of these ungainly weapons were in general service with the British Army.

muzzle velocity of 2,440 ft/sec its .303 round had great stopping power. Although only having a ten-round magazine, in skilled hands a high rate of fire was achieved of up to 15 rounds a minute. It was succeeded later during the war by the No. 4 Lee Enfield rifle, different only in the back sight and with an unpopular 'pig sticker' spike bayonet. Snipers, who made up an important element of every Commando unit, carried a standard SMLE rifle fitted with a telescopic sight.

The Thompson sub-machine gun, or 'Tommy-gun', capable of providing a devastating volume of fire at short range, became a weapon of choice for many Commandos given its great stopping power. A far higher proportion of these weapons were carried when compared to conventional units, normally issued to NCOs. Instead of drum magazines, which were prone to jamming, more reliable 20-round box magazines were employed that were also easier to carry in web equipment. Although Thompsons were retained in use until the end of the war, a growing number of the far simpler and cheaper mass-produced Sten machine carbines were carried in the field. Firing a 9mm bullet, it had a 32-round magazine. Although early models had a deservedly poor reputation for safety and reliability in the field, those produced later in the war performed well.

The Commando fighting troops had a far higher number of the highly effective .303 calibre gas-operated Bren light machine gun than regular units. It provided the main source of portable firepower used by the Commandos and could fire single rounds or full automatic bursts. Based on a Czech design developed at Brno and later manufactured at Enfield (hence the name), this extremely reliable automatic weapon weighed in at 23 lb and was fitted with a bipod for greater accuracy at ranges up to 550m. With a magazine of 30 rounds this highly accurate automatic weapon had a crew of two – one to fire the weapon and a second to carry further magazines filled with ammunition, tools, and spares. Several Bren guns were carried in each section, and with a practical rate of fire of 120 rounds a minute it was a powerful and highly accurate source of firepower. Indeed some thought it too accurate for an automatic weapon.

Types of grenade used by the Commandos included the No. 36 bomb or Mills bomb, No. 69 concussion grenade, and No. 77 phosphorous grenade used to produce a smoke screen, but also useful for clearing buildings or bunkers. Depending on the individual, No. 36 grenades could be thrown around 25 yards and were highly effective. Fitted with a discharger-cup and firing a ballistic cartridge, special SMLEs were retained to fire No. 36 grenades up to 200 yards.

The main source of immediate close-quarter indirect fire support at the disposal of Commando Troops was the lightweight standard and later parachute issue 2in. mortar, firing smoke, high-explosive and illumination rounds. This highly effective lightweight weapon consisted of little more than a short tube, a simple firing mechanism, and a base plate. It was operated hand-held with the spade or base plate firmly against the ground. A round was fired by dropping the shell down the short barrel, after which the angle was readjusted for the next shot. It had a maximum range of 500 yards, although it had far greater accuracy up to 300 yards.

Vickers MMGs in action during a night firing exercise at Achnacarry. (H32666)

HMS *Princess Beatrix*

This assault ship was built in 1939 as a civilian passenger ship and named *Princess Beatrix*. Along with her sister ship *Koningen Emma* she was engaged in carrying passengers across the North Sea between the Hook of Holland and Harwich. In 1940, she was requisitioned by the Ministry of War Transport, renamed HMS *Princess Beatrix* and converted to a troopship at Harland & Wolff's yards in Belfast. During the war years this vessel was heavily employed transporting Commandos as a dedicated assault ship, for example during the raids on the Lofoten Islands, Vaagso, and Dieppe. In 1946 *Princess Beatrix* was released from the Royal Navy to her former owners and, after refurbishing, resumed her route across the North Sea as a passenger ferry until she was scrapped.

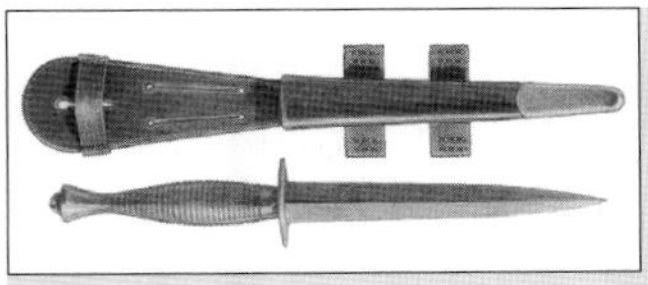

The Fairbairn-Sykes fighting knife
The Fairbairn-Sykes fighting knife in various patterns was carried by the Commandos throughout World War II. Designed, as the name implies, by Capt William Fairbairn and Capt Eric Sykes based on experience of close-quarter combat gained while serving as colonial policemen in Shanghai, it formed the primary hand-to-hand weapon used on raiding and other operations by the Commandos during World War II. A thrusting weapon primarily, with twin cutting edges, it could also be thrown if required. Initially, manufactured by Wilkinson Sword, a series of versions appeared during the war years with the Mk 3 becoming the model adopted for mass production. The Fairbairn-Sykes fighting knife was adapted as the shoulder emblem of the wartime Commandos and later Commando Association, as well as the shoulder flash of today's Royal Marine Commandos.

Early in the war the bolt-operated 0.55in. Boyes anti-tank rifle provided the Commandos with a man-portable anti-armour weapon. Its heavy weight (36 lb.), length (72in.), limited effectiveness against all but the most lightly armoured vehicle, and powerful recoil when fired made it an unpopular weapon from the start. The Boyes AT rifle was normally fired from the prone position and was also employed for house-breaking and against bunkers and emplacement. It was quickly discarded and replaced during 1943 with the PIAT (Projector Infantry Anti-Tank) firing a hollow-charge round effective up to 100 yards against most German armour. Its only drawback was the heavy weight of its bombs (2½ lb each), which meant only a limited number were carried by its two-man crew.

The Commandos initially lacked any crew-served support weapons in their war establishment, largely because of their weight and difficulty in manhandling them and their ammunition during raids. The effective and reliable water-cooled .303 Vickers medium machine gun and 3in. mortars were initially issued on an ad-hoc basis from a central reserve or else begged, borrowed or stolen from other units, to beef up firepower. During the Vaagso raid No. 3 Commando, for example, employed a borrowed 3in. mortar with great effect against the German garrison.

An improvised 3in. mortar team in action during the raid on Vaagso. (N532)

The formation of a support troop in each Commando in August 1943, equipped with the Vickers medium machine gun and 3in. mortar, provided at long last a source of sustained firepower on immediate call during combat. The tripod-mounted, belt-fed .303 Vickers MMG was capable of producing a greater volume of sustained small-arms fire than any other infantry weapon. It could fire at a rate up to 500 rounds a minute directly or indirectly at ranges up to 3,000 yards, but was extremely heavy at 88½ lb. It was operated by a crew of two men – one to fire the weapon and a second to ensure the smooth feeding of its belt of ammunition. A total of four men, however, were needed to move the gun, its tripod, ammunition, spare parts, and the water needed to cool the weapon.

The 3in. mortar fired smoke and HE bombs at high-trajectory into enemy positions. It consisted of a hollow tube with a firing pin at its bottom, a bipod stand, and heavy base plate to absorb recoil. This comparatively crude heavy weapon could be broken down and manhandled in three loads during an assault, but a major drawback was that each bomb weighed 10 lb. With a range of up to 2½ km and a maximum rate of 15 rounds a minute when used by a well-trained crew, it was a powerful source of indirect fire support.

Other weapons were issued on an ad-hoc basis. To beef up the firepower of Commando units during the Normandy landings, bipod-equipped Vickers K gas-operated LMGs, weighing in at 29½ lb, were also employed with 96-round drum magazines. To maintain surprise, the De Lisle Commando carbine was issued in small numbers, whose silencer enabled 'silent killing' up to a range of 400 yards. Occasionally the Lifebuoy personal flamethrower was also employed on active service. For the *Torch* operations No. 1 and No. 6 Commandos were issued with US uniforms, arms and equipment, given fears the French would be extremely hostile to troops in British uniform. The semi-automatic .30 M1 Garand rifles issued for this operation were eagerly retained by these units and employed by them for the rest of the war.

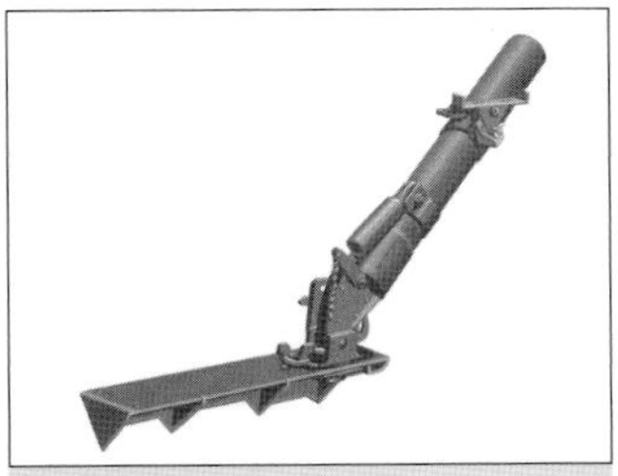

2in. mortar
The lightweight and extremely versatile 2in. mortar was widely employed by the British Army during World War II. Issued at platoon and section level, it provided infantry Commando fighting troops with a source of immediate, fast and flexible and indirect fire support, firing high-explosive, smoke and illumination rounds. A lightened version – omitting the base plate – was produced for the airborne forces during the war and also employed by the Commandos to beef up firepower and give them an ability to engage targets out of direct line of sight.

Command, control, communications and intelligence

Maj Gen Sir Robert 'Lucky' Laycock (1907–68), Chief of Combined Operations, talking to Royal Marine Commandos during an inspection, 1944. (H39029)

The effective planning, command and control of Commando raids always posed distinct problems for commanders. From the outset it was clear that for success they were always dependent on the input and coordination of and close cooperation between the three services – Army, Royal Air Force and the Royal Navy – for success. The Commandos were of course completely dependent on the senior service for transportation, landing them on a hostile shore and supporting them with naval gunfire if required during opposed landings, while the RAF provided vital aerial cover for landing operations and ensuing fighting, carried out supporting bombing raids on selected targets, and provided close air support on the battlefield. A joint command structure was clearly vital for success and had to rapidly be devised since nothing of its sort had previously existed in the UK during peacetime.

The initial responsibility for directing joint amphibious operations from the UK rested with Gen Sir Alan Bourne, Adjutant-General Royal Marines, who was appointed on 12 June 1940 as Commander, Offensive Operations (later retitled Director of Combined Operations), directly under the Chiefs of Staff and with his HQ at the Admiralty. His role was to coordinate the work of the three services, with an area of operations covering Norway, Holland, Belgium, and France. His brief included planning and executing operations as well as laying the foundations of a rapidly growing Combined Operations organization and training system. The Commandos were the only force directly under his command, although responsibility for organizing, training and equipping these units rested with the also newly formed MO9 section in the Directorate of Military Operations and Plans at the War Office (initially commanded by Lt Col Dudley Clarke). With Bourne still retaining his responsibilities as Adjutant-General, however, this seriously overburdened officer proved incapable of adequately carrying out both duties. On 17 July Churchill appointed Admiral of the Fleet Sir Roger

Special Service Brigade Advanced HQ order of battle

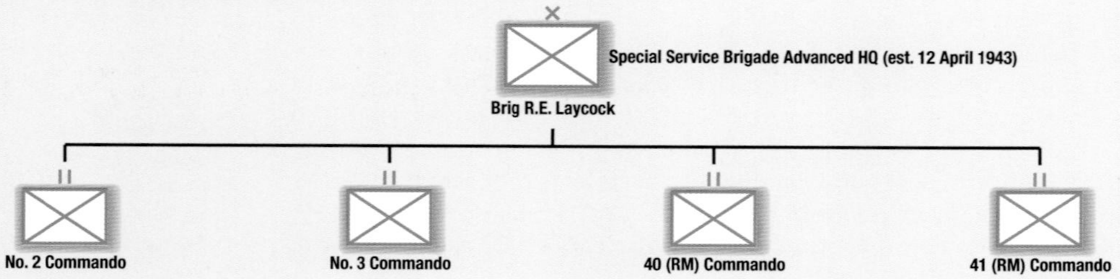
Special Service Brigade Advanced HQ (est. 12 April 1943)
Brig R.E. Laycock
No. 2 Commando
No. 3 Commando
40 (RM) Commando
41 (RM) Commando

Keyes as Director of Combined Operations (DCO), with Bourne acting as his deputy, to coordinate the work of the three services in devising, planning and carrying out both small-scale and large-scale amphibious operations. Based at a new HQ at Richmond Terrace in Whitehall, London, this distinguished 68-year-old veteran of the Gallipoli landings and the Zeebrugge Raid in April 1918 immediately set about organizing the Commandos, which formed his ground component and striking force directly under his command. Under Keyes, the staff of the Directorate of Combined Operations, drawn from all three services, was involved in gathering intelligence and planning work for potential operations against targets such as the Canary Islands, the Azores and Pantellaria in the Mediterranean, absorbing lessons from early raids and the failed attempt to seize Dakar from the Vichy French. A comprehensive Combined Operations training establishment quickly developed, moreover, as well as systems for developing, designing and building landing craft and other assorted specialized equipment required for large- and small-scale amphibious operations. The prickly and often autocratic Keyes resigned in October 1941, however, after a new directive and title as Adviser on Combined Operations given to him caused a major rift with the Chiefs of Staff.

The appointment of Cdre Lord Louis Mountbatten as Advisor on Combined Operations on 27 October 1941, with Maj Gen Charles Haydon acting as his Chief of Staff (formerly the OC Special Service Brigade), was an important milestone in the development of the Commandos and Combined Operations. His charismatic personality, skilled leadership and political sense worked wonders in terms of coordinating the three services. As Peter Young has written:

> It was a brilliant choice: Mountbatten was a man of forty-one. He had made a tremendous name for himself in command of the destroyer *Kelly*, which, after a splendid fighting career had been sunk off Crete earlier in the year.[18]

A new sense of drive and urgency was injected throughout the Combined Operations organization under this energetic, young and successful commander, who was responsible for collating intelligence, organizing raids, developing shipping and equipment, and planning for a large-scale amphibious invasion of Europe. A new structure for planning and the conduct of operations was developed and under his leadership the successful raids on Vaagso, Bruneval and St Nazaire were conducted between December 1941 and March 1942. In March 1942 he was made Chief of Combined Operations and promoted Vice Admiral, as well as being given the honorary ranks of

Special Service Brigade Rear HQ, order of battle, April 1943

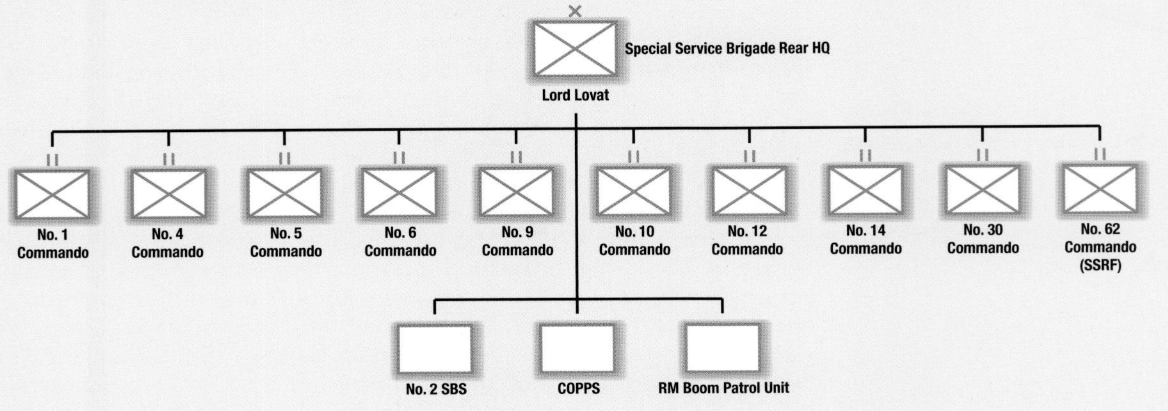
Special Service Brigade Rear HQ
Lord Lovat
No. 1 Commando
No. 4 Commando
No. 5 Commando
No. 6 Commando
No. 9 Commando
No. 10 Commando
No. 12 Commando
No. 14 Commando
No. 30 Commando
No. 62 Commando (SSRF)
No. 2 SBS
COPPS
RM Boom Patrol Unit

HM King George VI and Lord Lovat inspect Commandos before D-Day. (H18098)

Lieutenant-General and Air Marshal, and made a member of the Chiefs of Staff Committee. Under his command the Special Service Brigade grew in size, with the formation of the first Royal Marine Commandos, several specialist units and the centralization of Commando training at Achnacarry in the highlands of Scotland. Henceforward under Mountbatten and his successor Maj Gen Robert Laycock, COHQ became heavily involved in planning work by the Commander-in-Chief Home Forces for the invasion of North-West Europe, as well as the amphibious landings in North Africa, Sicily and Italy.

The formation of the HQ of the new Special Service Brigade in November 1940 led to the demise of MO9 of the Directorate of Military Operations and Plans and the resignation of Lt Col Dudley Clarke, who had overseen the formation of the Commandos. Under the initial command of Brig Charles Haydon, the Special Service Brigade prospered. Henceforward the Officer Commanding the Special Service Brigade was responsible for the day-to-day administration, organization, training, as well as the command and planning for raiding operations as directed by Combined Operations HQ. A signal platoon was quickly formed as part of the establishment of the Special Service Brigade's HQ, enabling it to command and control its widely distributed units. The despatch of increasingly large groups of Commandos overseas to various theatres of war, however, led to further changes in the command structure to ensure the Commandos received adequate representation in the planning and command of operations. In January 1941 an advanced HQ went overseas, commanded by Lt Col Robert Laycock, in charge of Nos. 7, 8 and 11 Commandos and attached troops. This hurriedly formed and hastily improvised HQ was intended for a specific operation and lacked the necessary resources. As the Brigade Major of the Special Service Brigade noted: 'You appear to be going to command a force of over 100 officers and 1,500 ORs with one staff officer, a note book and eight wireless sets which nobody can work.' The existence of this separate subordinate Commando HQ proved a short-lived and unsuccessful development and in most instances, however, Commando units in Force Z were parcelled out to other headquarters for all intents and purposes.

The concept of having a Commando HQ to coordinate Commandos when more than one unit was involved was tried unsuccessfully once again during Operation *Torch*, when a small HQ, commanded by Col Will Glendinning, Deputy Commander of the Special Service Brigade, and consisting of just two other officers, was formed. This proved less than successful since the Commandos were parcelled out to US units during the initial landings and during the latter stages of the campaign came under the command of individual formations, rendering it largely superfluous. The deployment of four

Commandos in the Mediterranean theatre in preparation for Operation *Husky* and the baleful experiences in Tunisia meant the expedient of temporarily forming a coordinating HQ was tried once again to ensure Commando interests were properly represented and their role understood by local commanders. A Special Service Brigade Advanced HQ was formed on 12 April 1943 at Prestwick (with Nos. 2, 3, 40 (RM) and 41 (RM) Commandos under command). During the planning for Operations *Husky* and *Avalanche* it worked in close cooperation with the senior HQs responsible for the planning and conduct of operations involving Commando units, in particular making them aware of the strengths, capabilities and limitations of its units and ensuring they were allocated appropriate tasks. A Rear HQ remained in the UK at Sherborne in Dorset, meanwhile, with responsibility for the remaining Commandos, No. 30 Commando, No. 62 Commando, No. 2 SBS, the COPPs and the RM Boom Patrol Unit.

The command and control of the Commandos was greatly improved by its general reorganization in mid 1943, since the existing Special Service Brigade HQ was badly overburdened in controlling so many units spread over such a wide geographical area. A new Special Service Group HQ was formed in its place, controlling four new subordinate Special Service Brigades, as well as various other attached specialist units. The functions of the new Special Service Group HQ were mainly administrative, dealing with pay, organization and the training of its formations and, to a far lesser extent, planning. It was not designed to work in the field, although individual members of its staff helped its subordinate formations with planning of operations. Even so, a detached tactical HQ of the Special Service Group, commanded by Brig John Durnford-Slater, was attached to the HQ of 2nd British Army, to ensure Commando interests were safeguarded during the D-Day landings. Each Special Service Brigade HQ, with its own attached Signal Platoon, was an operational HQ and commanded and administered four Commandos in the field. The formation of individual Special Service Brigades, as part of the Special Service Group organization, to a large degree addressed concerns that the role and capabilities of the Commandos was greatly misunderstood by higher-formation HQs and therefore misemployed. At last they ensured Commandos had an adequate representation and say in operations, while under the command of higher HQs outside of the UK. Indeed, by the end of the war the Special Service Group HQ had only a few specialist units under its command, together with those formations and units briefly returning to the UK for rest and retraining from North-West Europe.

HM King George VI talks to Lt Col Peter Young. (H38749)

The hazards of Commando life: a member of the HQ of 4th Special Service Brigade disembarks in a somewhat unorthodox manner from an LCI(S) on Nan Red Beach, Normandy, 6 June 1944. (B5219)

The senior officer in each Commando held the rank of lieutenant-colonel, and was assisted by a relatively small staff, particularly weak on the administrative side. A single officer was responsible for security and intelligence work, heading up a small sub-section in each Commando consisting of one officer, two NCOs and three ORs responsible for gathering, collating and disseminating the latest information. The intelligence officer regularly attended briefings at COHQ, and his section often played a critical role, since raids were often dependent on knowledge of enemy strength, dispositions, defences, and terrain. A signals platoon always formed part of each HQ, equipped with standard British radio equipment (wireless sets No. 19 and No. 48) of World War II, line and visual signalling equipment such as semaphore, flags, heliographs and Verey pistols. These were vital for intercommunication with higher HQs and supporting arms and services. The No. 18 set was a medium-range radio carried on the back, which was an improvement over the short-range No. 38 also used by the Commandos, worn clipped onto webbing on the chest. Later the No. 46 wireless set was widely employed, which weighed in at over 30 lb. including batteries and a junction box carried by each operator in a pack. Used in a manpack role it had a range of four miles, but if rigged as a ground station it was considerably further. Like other specialists on operations, signallers would be detached to fighting troops for intercommunication purposes. The small size of each Commando and its comparatively few sub-units facilitated command, control and communication, except when widely dispersed. In any event, command responsibility was devolved down to junior officers, NCOs and men, who were expected to exercise a degree of leadership, initiative and responsibility unknown in regular units. A heavy reliance was placed on runners during raiding operations given the unreliability and sheer weight of standard issue RT sets used by the British Army, as well as the fluidity of the fighting. Flare pistols were also standard issue for both illumination and signalling.

Combat operations

Operation *Ambassador*: Guernsey, July 1940

The pressure to mount a raid against German-occupied Europe using the new Commandos quickly mounted during the summer of 1940, not least from Prime Minister Winston Churchill. Attention quickly turned to the Channel Islands, the only part of the UK to fall under the German jackboot. In a memorandum written by the Prime Minister on 2 July he observed:

> If it be true that a few hundred German troops have landed on Jersey or Guernsey by troop-carriers, plans should be studied to land secretly by night on the Islands and kill or capture the invaders. This is exactly one of the exploits for which the Commandos would be suited.[19]

Following the endorsement of the War Cabinet, planning to mount a raid on Guernsey quickly went forward, with the aim being to land three separate parties on the southern coast of the island. One hundred and forty men drawn from No. 3 Commando and No. 11 Independent Company were hurriedly selected. On 14/15 June Operation *Ambassador* was mounted with the objective of killing Germans troops, capturing prisoners, and attacking German aircraft and installations on the recently occupied airfield. A small flotilla consisting of two destroyers – HMS *Scimitar* and HMS *Saladin* – transported the Commando and men of the Independent Company across the Channel, who were then transhipped into six RAF air-sea rescue launches for the final approach to the shore.

Royal Marines of No. 48 (RM) Commando being briefed by an NCO. (A28413)

The parties from No. 11 Independent Company failed to land as two RAF launches broke down and navigational errors occurred. Only a 40-man fighting troop from No. 3 Commando, led personally by Lt Col John Durnford-Slater, actually made it to dry land in Houlin Houet Bay by wading through the surf (the shore was too rocky). Tasked with making a diversion for No. 11 Independent Company's attack on the airfield, patrols were immediately sent out, a roadblock established and a search made of the Jerbourg Peninsula for German troops. No contact was made, however, with the enemy. A re-embarkation was ordered by Durnford-Slater, but heavy rollers crashing on the beach meant that most of the Commandos had to swim out to the RAF launches waiting 100 yards offshore. Three men unable to swim failed in the attempt and despite plans to recover them two days later, they eventually fell into enemy hands.

The Guernsey raid was a fiasco that achieved few results. It earned a fierce rebuke from the Prime Minister, who ordered that there be 'no more silly fiascos like those perpetrated at Guernsey'. The lessons of the raid were all too clear to participants. As Durnford-Slater later admitted:

> Looking back, I can see that under such rushed conditions, with no experience, no proper landing craft or training, this first operation was foredoomed to failure. Later the word Commando became synonymous with perfectly trained, tough, hard-fighting and skilled specialists. You don't achieve this overnight.[20]

It did provide valuable experience and emphasized the need for careful planning, in particular with lessons being learnt about landing troops at the right location and the unsuitability of crash boats for landing operations on a hostile shore. It had been a disappointing failure, largely because of poor planning, inadequate resources, and insufficient training.

Operation *Claymore*: the 1941 raid on the Lofoten Islands

The Lofoten Islands, lying off the Norwegian mainland and 100 miles inside the Arctic Circle, contained various military and economic objectives, and thus were chosen as the objective for the first large-scale Commando raid – Operation *Claymore* – mounted from the United Kingdom during World War II. The plan developed by COHQ and the Special Service Brigade had both a naval and ground component. The 6th Destroyer Flotilla (consisting of HMS *Somali*, HMS *Bedouin*, HMS *Tartar*, HMS *Legion* and HMS *Eskimo*), commanded by Capt C. Caslon, was tasked with escorting a landing force to and from the Lofotens, as well as giving naval support if and when required to the landings. Under the overall command of Brig Charles Haydon, No. 3 and No. 4 Special Service Battalions, with an attached party of 50 Free Norwegian sailors, were tasked with

Operation *Claymore* (ground component)

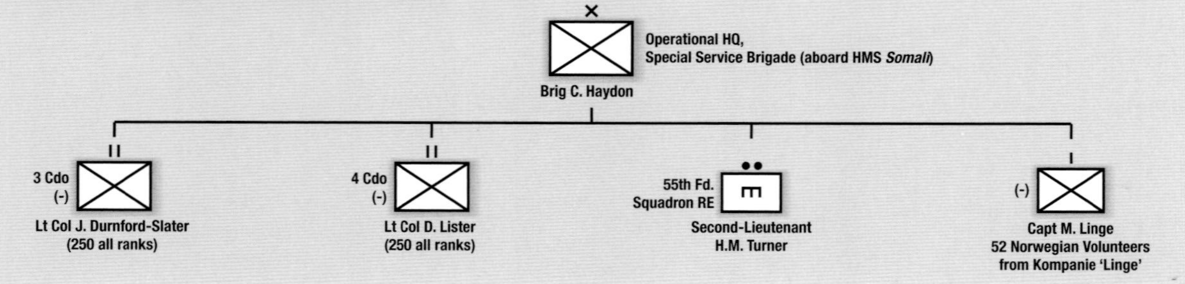

Operational HQ,
Special Service Brigade (aboard HMS Somali)
Brig C. Haydon
3 Cdo
(-)
Lt Col J. Durnford-Slater
(250 all ranks)
4 Cdo
(-)
Lt Col D. Lister
(250 all ranks)
55th Fd. Squadron RE
Second-Lieutenant
H.M. Turner
(-)
Capt M. Linge
52 Norwegian Volunteers
from Kompanie 'Linge'

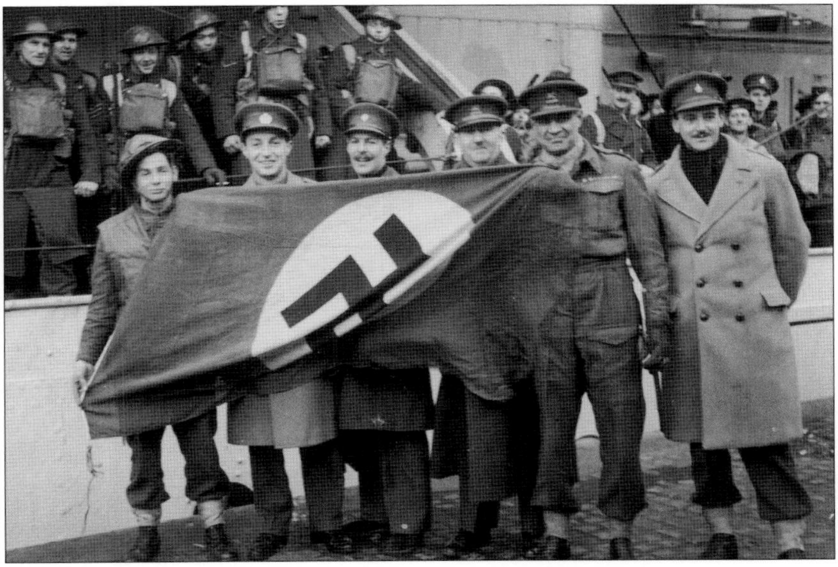

A group of British officers display a captured Nazi flag following the Lofoten raid. (N419)

destroying fish oil factories (producing glycerine used in German munitions and for making vitamin supplements), sinking enemy shipping, and bringing back prisoners and volunteers for the Free Norwegian forces. Several naval demolition parties also accompanied the landing force. The plan involved simultaneous landings on the key ports on the Lofoten Islands: Stamsund, Henningsvaer, Brettesness, and the capital Svolvaer. With only 50 Germans reported in the area, only light resistance was anticipated. No. 3 Special Service Battailon would land at Stamsund and Henningsvaer, while No. 4 Special Service Battailon attacked Brettesness and the capital Svolvaer.

The two assault ships carrying the ground component of Operation *Claymore* left Gourock on 21 February for Scapa Flow in the Orkney Islands, where further training, planning and familiarization with the RN warships was carried out. On 1 March 1941 a small flotilla – codenamed Force 'Rebel' – consisting of the 6th Destroyer Flotilla and the assault ships HMS *Queen Emma* and HMS *Beatrix*, with the now re-designated No. 3 and 4 Commandos aboard, left Scapa Flow on its three-day-long voyage to Norway. Foul weather en route caused widespread seasickness amongst the troops, however, and a German reconnaissance aircraft spotted the ships, although no action was taken to intercept them or alert possible landing sites.

The lights of the ports and navigational beacons were still blazing when early in the morning of 4 March the British flotilla arrived off the Lofoten Islands. Without further ado landing craft from HMS *Queen Emma* and HMS *Beatrix* quickly disembarked the assault troops onshore without a hitch, despite the intense cold. An armed German trawler – the *Krebs* – leaving the harbour at Sramsund, however, was quickly engaged and put out of action by HMS *Somali*. Surprise was near complete and the small German garrison and various civilians quickly surrendered without firing a shot. A very warm welcome was received from the local Norwegian population, some of whom thought the troops approaching were part of a German training exercise; they were delighted to see British forces and eager to assist in any way. Cups of ersatz coffee were quickly distributed to all those within reach. All the fish oil factories were rapidly destroyed, ships in harbour sunk, and military installations blown up. With their tasks completed the Commando assault force re-embarked by 1300 hours and departed for the UK. The only sign of the German Luftwaffe was spotted just before darkness when a single reconnaissance aircraft circled the departing convoy.

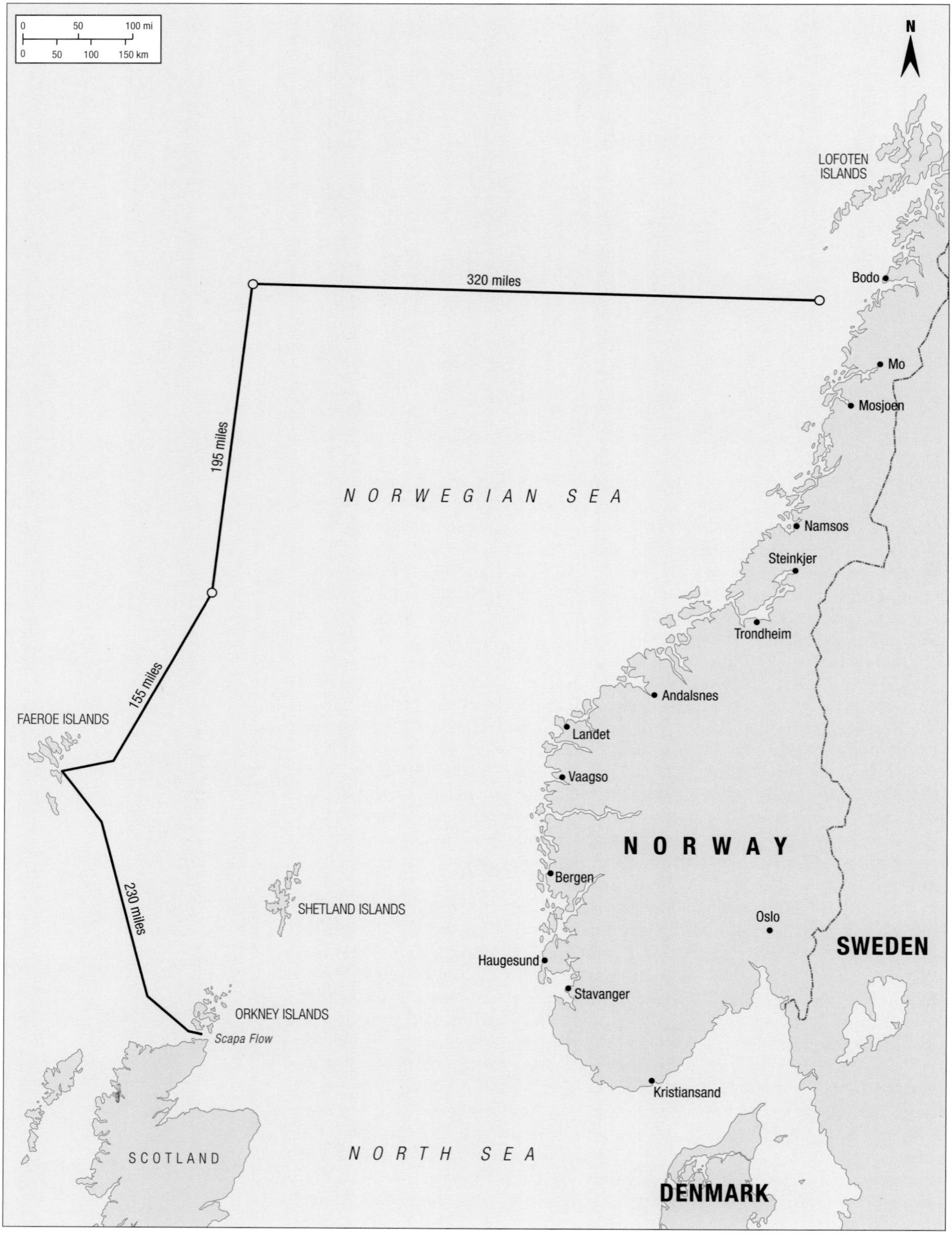
0
50
100 mi
0
50
100
150 km
N
LOFOTEN ISLANDS
Bodo
320 miles
Mo
Mosjoen
195 miles
NORWEGIAN SEA
Namsos
Steinkjer
Trondheim
Andalsnes
155 miles
FAEROE ISLANDS
Landet
Vaagso
NORWAY
Bergen
230 miles
SHETLAND ISLANDS
Oslo
SWEDEN
Haugesund
Stavanger
ORKNEY ISLANDS
Scapa Flow
Kristiansand
SCOTLAND
NORTH SEA
DENMARK

The route taken to the Lofoten Islands from Scapa Flow during Operation *Claymore*.

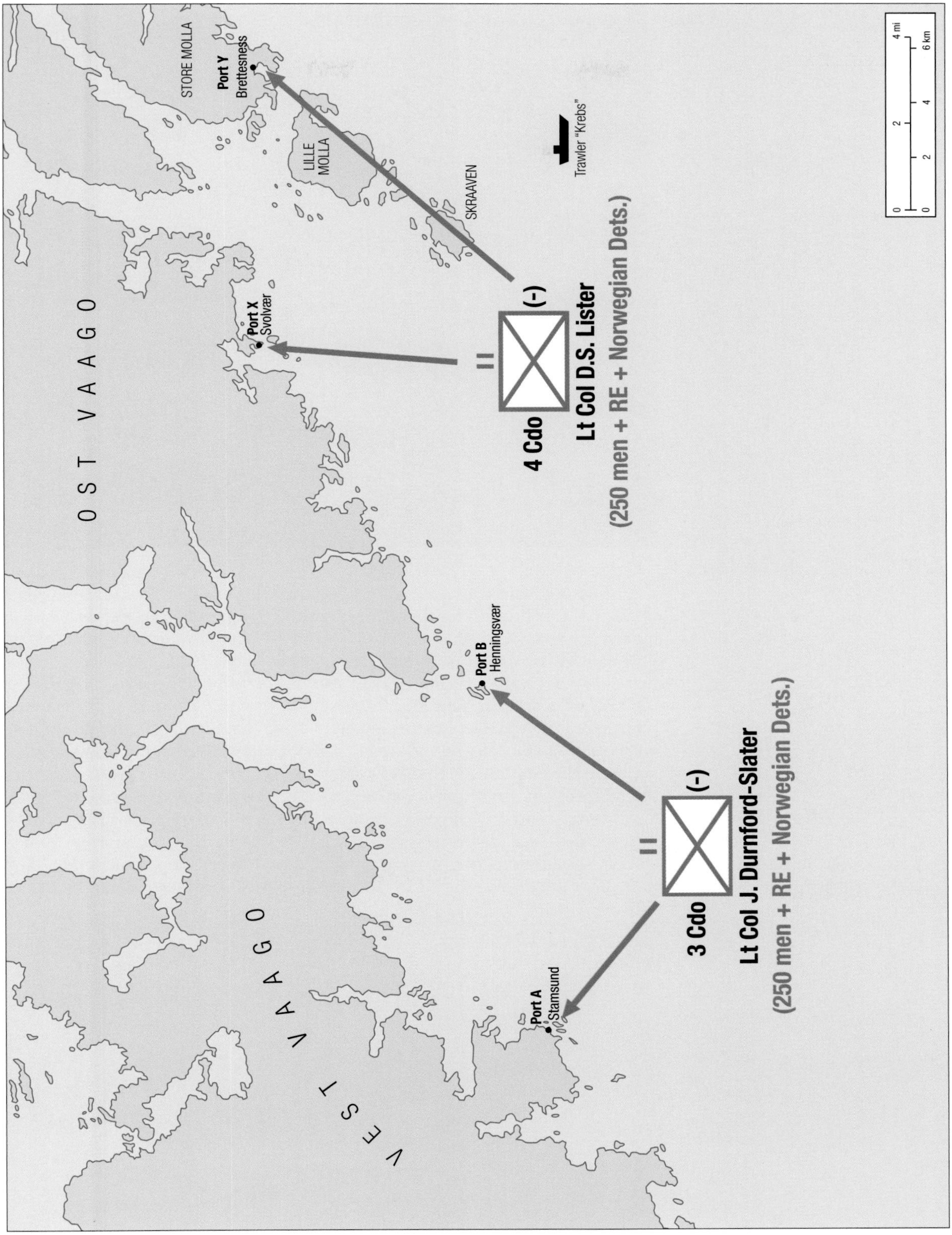

OST VAAGO
VEST VAAGO
STORE MOLLA
Port Y
Brettesness
LILLE MOLLA
SKRAAVEN
Trawler "Krebs"
Port X
Svolvær
4 Cdo
(-)
Lt Col D.S. Lister
(250 men + RE + Norwegian Dets.)
Port B
Henningsvær
3 Cdo
(-)
Lt Col J. Durnford-Slater
(250 men + RE + Norwegian Dets.)
Port A
Stamsund
0 2 4 mi
0 2 4 6 km

The landings of Nos. 3 and 4 Commandos in the Lofotens.

A line of MLC cruising at sea during the Lofoten Islands raid. (N437)

The Lofoten raid was a great success for the Commandos who had languished in the UK for months without action, although for some the lack of German opposition was a distinct anti-climax. 18 fish oil factories were set ablaze; 20,000 tons of shipping was sunk in the harbour; and nearly a million gallons of oil and petrol were set alight. A total of 315 volunteers for the Norwegian armed forces in exile, 60 suspected 'Quisling' collaborators and 225 German prisoners were returned to the UK. The English manager of Messrs Allen & Hanbury, who had been caught in Norway by the German invasion, was liberated to his great relief and transported home. Perhaps of greater significance than the visible results of the raid, which received widespread publicity, was the fact that some rotors for a top-secret German 'Enigma' code machine were captured aboard the *Krebs*; these helped the code-breakers of Bletchley Park to break key, top secret German ciphers. Apart from one British casualty – an officer who accidentally shot himself in the thigh with his own sidearm – British losses were nil. The British

HMS *Queen Emma* during the Lofoten Islands raid. (N429)

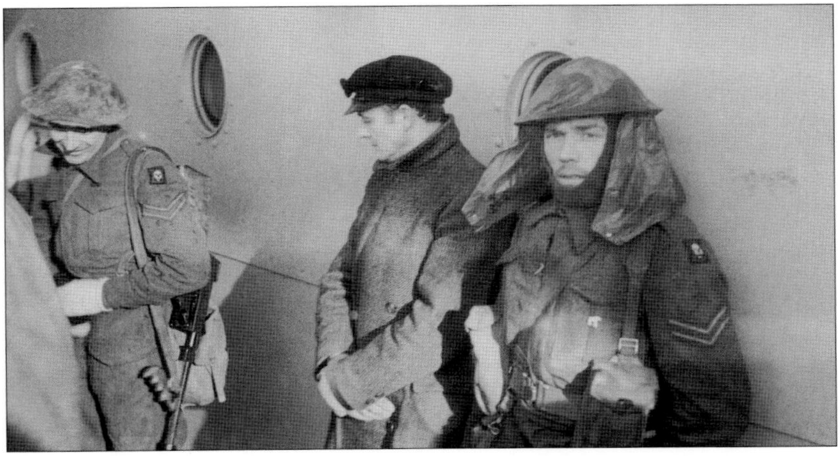

A Commando guards a suspect 'Quisling' following the raid on the Lofoten Islands. (N417)

press seized upon the raid, news of which was greeted with considerable pride by the public still starved of success. To cap it all, a cheeky British officer – Lt R.L. Wills – purportedly telegrammed Adolf Hitler from the Telegraph Office at Stamsund: 'You said in your last speech that German troops would meet the British wherever they landed. Where are your troops?'

Operations *Anklet* and *Archery*: the 1941 raid on Vaagso

The lengthy shoreline of Norway was again chosen for a further large-scale raid during 1941, with planning for an attack on the small Norwegian port of South Vaagso, located on the north shore of Nordfjord and commanding the entrance to a system of other fjords, undertaken only two months after Lord Louis Mounbatten took over as Chief of Combined Operations from Adm Keyes. This small port and naval anchorage, lying between Bergen and Trondheim, was garrisoned by approximately 200 troops belonging to the German 181st Division, who had a single tank in support in the town. A four-gun coastal battery on Maaloy Island – equipped with four Belgian 75mm guns – dominated the approach to the port, while other coastal defence batteries and anti-aircraft guns were located nearby, although not all could bear on the immediate vicinity of the port. This raid was a much more ambitious operation than anything attempted before, and was directed against a defended area; it was therefore likely to provoke a stiff German reaction. As one officer put it: 'At long last we would learn if our training had made us the fighting and killing force we were intended to be.'[21] It had the immediate objective of attacking and eliminating the German garrison and military installations, and, like that of the Lofoten Islands, destroying fish oil factories used in munitions production, sinking hostile shipping, gathering intelligence, and lastly returning Norwegian volunteers and suspected Quislings to the UK. In the longer term, moreover, it was hoped the threat demonstrated by this raid and potential future operations in Norway would tie down large numbers of German troops, and further reinforcements, badly needed in other theatres of war, would be diverted to help garrison Norway against future attacks.

Lord Louis Mountbatten inspects men of No. 3 Commando shortly before they depart on the Vaagso raid. (N504)

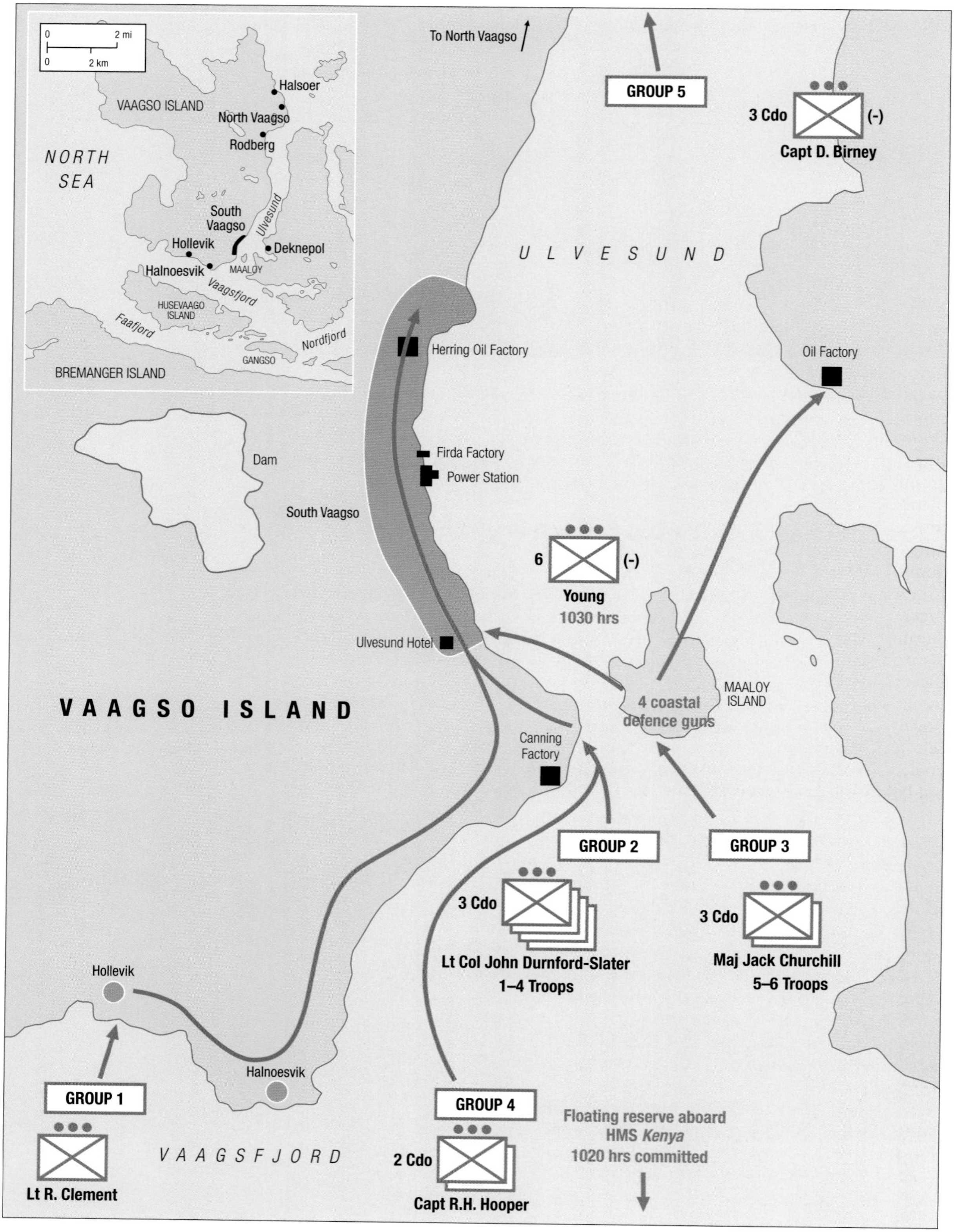

0
2 mi
0
2 km
Halsoer
VAAGSO ISLAND
North Vaagso
Rodberg
NORTH
SEA
South
Vaagso
Ulvesund
Hollevik
Deknepol
Halnoesvik
MAALOY
Vaagsfjord
HUSEVAAGO
ISLAND
Faafjord
Nordfjord
GANGSO
BREMANGER ISLAND
To North Vaagso
GROUP 5
3 Cdo
(-)
Capt D. Birney
ULVESUND
Herring Oil Factory
Oil Factory
Dam
Firda Factory
Power Station
South Vaagso
6
(-)
Young
1030 hrs
Ulvesund Hotel
VAAGSO ISLAND
4 coastal
defence guns
MAALOY
ISLAND
Canning
Factory
GROUP 2
GROUP 3
3 Cdo
Lt Col John Durnford-Slater
1–4 Troops
3 Cdo
Maj Jack Churchill
5–6 Troops
Hollevik
Halnoesvik
GROUP 1
GROUP 4
Floating reserve aboard
HMS Kenya
1020 hrs committed
VAAGSFJORD
2 Cdo
Capt R.H. Hooper
Lt R. Clement

The raid on Vaagso.

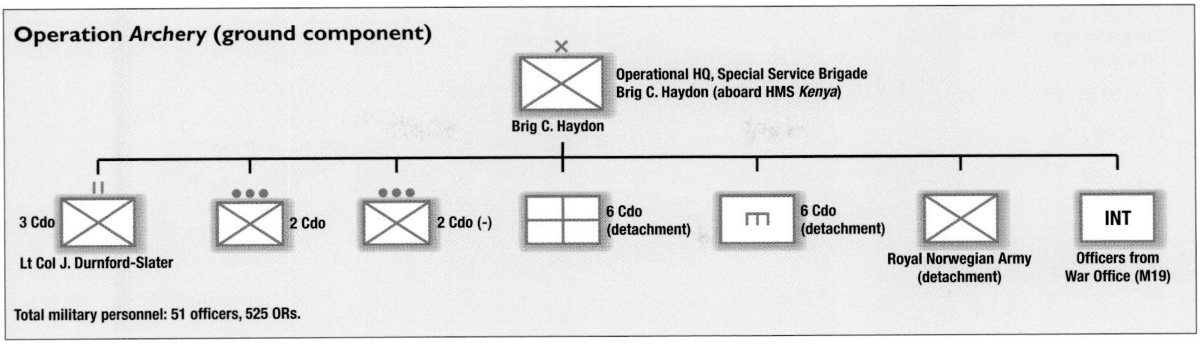
Operation Archery (ground component)
Operational HQ, Special Service Brigade
Brig C. Haydon (aboard HMS Kenya)
Brig C. Haydon
3 Cdo
Lt Col J. Durnford-Slater
2 Cdo
2 Cdo (-)
6 Cdo (detachment)
6 Cdo (detachment)
Royal Norwegian Army (detachment)
INT
Officers from War Office (M19)
Total military personnel: 51 officers, 525 ORs.

The overall command of the attack on South Vaagso was given to Adm Sir John Tovey, Commander-in-Chief Home Fleet, whose heavy warships provided distant cover for the raid. The joint force commanders for Operation *Archery* were appointed on 9 December, with R Adm H.M. Burroughs chosen as the naval commander and Brig Charles Haydon as army commander. A task force consisting of HMS *Kenya* (a 6in. gun cruiser), four escorting destroyers (HMS *Onslow*, *Oribi*, *Offa* and *Chiddingfold*), HM Submarine *Tuna* and two landing ships – HMS *Prince Charles* and HMS *Prince Leopold* – carried and supported the ground forces during the landings. A mixed force of RAF Hampden and Blenheim bombers, drawn from Bomber Command and Coastal Command, provided close air support and would also neutralize enemy airfields within range of Vaagso; additionally, long-range Beaufighters and Blenheim fighter-bombers provided top cover for the landings, shipping lying offshore, and Commandos operating on land. The ground component detailed for Operation *Archery* consisted of 51 officers and 525 ORs, commanded by Lt Col John Durnford-Slater, OC No. 3 Commando; the men were drawn from No. 3 Commando, two troops of No. 2 Commando, and medical and engineer detachments from No. 4 and No. 6 Commandos. Smaller detachments of intelligence personnel, press photographers, film crews, and men from the Royal Norwegian Army, who acted as guides and interpreters, were also selected. Meticulous planning was again the order of the day for the main landings, with numerous rehearsals and intensive specialized training carried out before the force was despatched for the raid. A carefully planned small-scale

Maj Jack Churchill inspects a captured coastal defence gun during the Vaagso raid. (N463)

An injured Commando having his wounds dressed during the Vaagso raid. (N477)

diversion, moreover, dubbed Operation *Anklet*, was also planned, involving 300 men of No. 12 Commando who would raid the Lofoten Islands once again. The plan of attack on South Vaagso involved four separate landings in and around the port. To prevent German reinforcements reaching the port once the raid was underway, one group of Commandos would land north of the town and block the coast road at Rodberg. 200 men would deal with the town itself and another smaller group would neutralize the coastal battery on Maaloy Island, which dominated the area. A fourth much smaller group would capture a German strongpoint at Hollevik south of the town and then act as a reserve. Finally, a fifth group consisting of two fighting troops of No. 2 Commando would remain aboard ship acting as a floating reserve in case of any difficulties. On 13 December the force embarked for Scapa Flow, where further training and meticulous preparations were carried out. As one officer recorded:

> With maps, air photographs and models every single man was shown his task and a variety of possible alternatives: every man was to be sure he understood his role.[22]

106

British wounded being evacuated to an ALC during the attack on Vaagso. (N481)

On Christmas Eve the assault flotilla left for Sollum Voe in the Shetland Islands. Bad weather, however, caused a further 24-hour delay, in order to repair damage aboard various ships – many of which were not designed for the North Sea. HMS *Prince Charles*, for example, shipped 145 tons of water and suffered damage to her superstructure.

The assault force departed on its 300-mile-long voyage to Norway on Boxing Day, with capital ships of the Home Fleet, commanded by Adm Sir John Tovey, providing distant cover in North Sea, while another smaller flotilla moved northwards towards the Lofoten Islands.

A line of ALCs moves towards the Norwegian shoreline during the raid on Vaagso. (N496)

The small-scale diversionary attack – Operation *Anklet* – went like clockwork. 300 men of No. 12 Commando and a small group from the free Royal Norwegian Army, under the overall command of Lt Col S.S. Harrison, landed on the Lofoten Islands on 26 December where they caught the tiny German garrison completely by surprise. As planned the towns of Reine and Moskenes were quickly occupied, small German installations destroyed and both the small garrison and Norwegian collaborators taken into custody. As intended it successfully diverted German attention from central Norway and disrupted naval traffic in the area. The small assault force remained for two days until a near miss by a German bomb on HMS *Arethusa* persuaded its captain of the wisdom of departing, since his small fleet lacked any air cover. They left carrying with them the raiding force, German prisoners and suspected Quislings.

The attack on South Vaagso and its environs was to prove a far sterner test of the Commandos than the minor raids that had gone before, and Operation *Anklet*. The seaborne approach to the objective across the North Sea passed without incident, with the weather gradually improving en route. HMS *Tuna*, acting as a navigational beacon, guided the assault force to the entrance of Vaagsford just as RAF bombers began their bombing runs.

The landing itself began at 0700 hours on 27 December, when the assault force entered the fjord. A fierce naval bombardment of Maaloy Island and its coastal battery by HMS *Kenya* and three destroyers immediately began. Under the cover of this shelling and a smoke screen laid by low-flying Hampden and Blenheim bombers, the main body of No. 3 Commando – four fighting troops

An impromptu conference being held on Maaloy Island before reinforcements were sent to Vaagso town. (N498)

A group of Commandos advance up the main street in Vaagso. (N515)

– quickly transhipped from HMS *Prince Leopold* and HMS *Prince Charles* into Assault Landing Craft, and landed at various points in and around South Vaagso. They planned to cut the port off from outside support and eliminate enemy strongpoints. Overhead Beaufighters and Blenheim long-range fighters provided air cover for the landing force, making round trips of 650km from airbases at Wick in Scotland or 400km from the Shetland Islands.

The initial landings made by No. 3 Commando went well, with the bombardment by HMS *Kenya* lifting when the ALC carrying the assault force were just 50m from the beach. Fire then switched to the Rugsundo battery, which was quickly neutralized, although it resumed intermittent fire throughout the day. The coastal battery on Maaloy Island posed the great threat to the landings. Two troops of Commandos quickly landed and overran the battery in just 20 minutes, with Maj Jack Churchill, brandishing a Claymore sword in hand, leading the way. Its surprised defenders, stunned by the shock and ferocity of the initial bombardment, offered only limited resistance. As planned the Commandos took the surviving garrison prisoner, demolished the guns, and a small party was detached and landed unopposed nearby to destroy a fish oil factory at Mortenses. The Hollevik landings, 2km south of South Vaagso, encountered no opposition whatsoever. Apart from two seriously wounded German marines caught by the initial naval bombardment, the remainder of the garrison had decamped to South Vaagso for breakfast. The fifth group were carried aboard HMS *Oribi* into Ulvesund, after it was confirmed that the Maaloy battery had fallen into British hands, and landed to the north of South Vaagso. They landed without opposition and cratered the road to prevent German reinforcements reaching the town.

The main body of No. 3 Commando attacking South Vaagso, however, fared less well. A phosphorous smoke bomb dropped by a badly damaged Hampden aircraft, hit by anti-aircraft fire from an armed German trawler in Ulvesund during the initial landing, caused heavy losses amongst men of 4 Troop crammed tightly into one ALC. The remaining Commandos landed unopposed at the foot of a low cliff nearby the town as planned, shielded by the smokescreen, and rapidly scaled the cliff. The advance into South Vaagso by the leading Commandos, personally led by Lt Col John Durnford-Slater, immediately began. This small port consisted of a single ¾-mile-long street running parallel to the shore flanked on either side by wooden houses, factories and warehouses. A range of snow-covered mountains to one side and the sea to the other prevented any attempts at outflanking the defenders. The leading troops met strong resistance from a larger than anticipated German infantry garrison (an additional party of 50 men had just arrived in town on Christmas leave), many of whom had fought in the Norwegian campaign. These combat veterans quickly converted many buildings and warehouses along the waterfront into strongpoints that had to be winkled out one by one. The house-to-house fighting required to clear these men caused serious casualties with German snipers hidden in the buildings and on the hillsides above inflicting further heavy losses, especially amongst British officers. The Royal Navy was also engaged offshore in Ulvesund, after the guns on Maaloy had been neutralized. Under cover provided by the RAF, HMS *Oribi* and HMS *Onslow* destroyed enemy shipping in the anchorage, most of which had already been scuttled by the Germans to prevent capture, and seized vital codebooks off the *Fohn*, a German armed trawler that had just arrived in Ulvesund.

The strength of German resistance encountered in South Vaagso, whose garrison displayed considerable combat skill, good marksmanship and dogged courage throughout the fighting, and rapidly escalating casualties meant progress fell far short of what had been anticipated, with the attack stalled around an enemy strongpoint centred on the Ulvesund Hotel. A 3in. mortar, not part of the official war establishment of No. 3 Commando and gained by 'private enterprise', provided some covering fire for the advancing Commandos, but it was not enough on its own to neutralize the defenders. Further reinforcements from the floating reserve held aboard ship – two fighting troops of No. 2 Commando – and other men diverted after completing their assigned tasks at Hollevik and Maaloy Island, were committed at 1020 hours, giving the attack added impetus. No. 6 Troop from Maaloy joined the main party, moreover, and quickly got the main attack moving again, while the floating reserve landed at the south end of the town at the original landing site. By 1345 hours South Vaagso had been cleared after fierce fighting, and an hour later, having completed demolition work on fish oil factories, gun batteries, warehouses, a lighthouse, barracks and telephone exchanges, the force withdrew. By 1434 the troops were all back aboard ship.

The raid on South Vaagso had been a great success, carried out after careful planning and rehearsal and executed with great skill by all three services – despite the fierce resistance offered by the local garrison. Although only a comparatively small-scale, limited operation it ended 1941 on a high note and established Mountbatten's reputation as the Chief of Combined Operations. It also reflected the growing skill and expertise in mounting amphibious raids

A group of three Commandos engaged in house-to-house fighting in Vaagso town. (N530)

involving the close cooperation of all three arms of service, including the specialized skills of landing on rocky shorelines and scaling cliffs. It bore out the training given to the Commandos. As one participant later recorded:

> Vaagso was ... a minor classic of amphibious warfare. A raid which, despite the multitudinous accidents inseparable from warfare, actually went according to plan, in that all the groups into which the force was divided carried out their assigned tasks.[23]

Much had been learnt by the Commandos from the raid, including the need for specialized instruction in street fighting. Some 15,630 tons of shipping was destroyed, several German aircraft downed near the town, and airfields at Herdia and Stavanger badly damaged. A notable intelligence coup was the capture aboard the *Fohn* of codebooks and other papers that gave the Royal Navy call signs for enemy ships and various challenges, countersigns and emergency signals. The 'butcher's bill' for Operation *Archery* had fortunately been light, with just 20 Commandos killed and a further 57 wounded during the pitched fighting ashore. The Royal Navy also lost two killed and six wounded, and damage had been inflicted on several ships. Several planes were downed. A total of 15,000 tons of enemy shipping was destroyed, as well as fish oil processing plants, storehouses and dockyards used by the German garrison. Over 100 German prisoners and four Quislings returned to the UK along with 77 new recruits for the Free Norwegian Army. It was estimated 150 German soldiers were killed during the fighting. As hoped by the British, soon after operations *Anklet* and *Archery* major German reinforcements were deployed in Norway to shore up the defences against further raids.

'The greatest raid of all': Operation *Chariot* – No. 2 Commando at St Nazaire, 1942

The port of St Nazaire, located on the Atlantic seaboard of France six miles up the estuary of the River Loire, was selected as a target for a Commando raid early in 1942. It possessed the only dry dock of a size capable of repairing German capital ships operating against the UK's sea lines of communication in the Atlantic. The primary objective of Operation *Chariot* was the destruction of this huge dry dock, without which any damaged large German warships would have no alternative other than returning to home waters for repair; the remaining port installations and U-Boat pens formed secondary targets. A major difficulty facing an attack force, however, was that St Nazaire was situated six miles up the treacherous River Loire, on its northern shore, with only a single deep water channel running through shoals and mud-flats navigable by larger ships.

Lt Col Charles Newman, who commanded the ground component of Operation *Chariot*. (HU 16542)

The strategic significance of the port of St Nazaire was not lost to the German high command. and its installations and new U-Boat base were heavily defended against seaborne and aerial attack. Unsurprisingly, the narrow Charpentier Channel was dominated by a series of coastal batteries, manned by 280th Naval Artillery Battalion, located along the northern and southern shores. These included two 240mm railway guns near La Pouligern and six fixed heavy coastal batteries with guns ranging from 75mm to 170mm in calibre. In closer proximity to St Nazaire and in and around the port itself were three battalions of the 22nd Naval Flak Brigade, commanded by Kapitain zur See Karl-Konrad Mecke, equipped with 43 anti-aircraft guns ranging from 20 to 40mm in calibre, capable of being used in a dual role. Several batteries of powerful searchlights were positioned to sweep the estuary if required. The local defence of St Nazaire, under the command of Harbour Commander Kellerman, consisted of guard companies armed with light weapons and several harbour defence vessels, backed up by naval technicians of 2 and 4 Work Companies, workers from

Organization Todt, U-Boat maintenance staff, and the crews of various ships in the port. In addition to these 5,000 assorted second-line troops, a regiment of 133rd Infantry Division was garrisoned nearby, although it was not held at immediate readiness to move into the port if an attack occurred.

The primary task of destroying the Normandie dock fell to the Royal Navy, since it was impossible to bring a slow-moving ALC in close enough to employ a large Commando force. Instead, an elderly ex-US Navy destroyer HMS *Campbeltown* (formerly the USS *Buchanan*) was tasked with ramming the outer caisson of the Normandie dock. A timed fuse would then detonate depth charges containing high explosive several hours later, destroying both the dock gates and other installations within its immediate vicinity. To provide an element of surprise and confuse the enemy, this Lend Lease destroyer was lightened and modified structurally to resemble a German *Mowe* class destroyer. It was also fitted with armour plates on deck to protect troops carried aboard. HMS *Campbeltown* would approach flying a German flag as a *ruse de guerre*. Furthermore German naval codebooks captured at Vaagso would help deceive the enemy if the shore batteries challenged the warship. The attention of the Germans, moreover, was to be diverted away from the estuary of the Loire by Bomber Command launching bombing raids in the surrounding area.

The ground component of Operation *Chariot* was tasked with destroying other port and naval installations in the area. Under the command of Lt Col Charles Newman, 200 men from No. 2 Commando were selected to undertake Operation *Chariot*, with small demolition parties drawn from Nos. 1, 3, 4, 5, 9 and 12 Commandos attached. A large detachment of Commandos were to be carried aboard HMS *Campbeltown*, with further troops transported aboard a dozen flimsy, wooden Fairmile B motor launches, which lacked any real form of protection. The attacking force would be split into three parts, with the first landing at the Old Mole, the second near the Old Entrance to the dock and a third disembarking off HMS *Campbeltown* after it rammed the entrance gate to the Normandie dock. Each small striking force was divided into three groups: assault troops would destroy enemy defences and establish a defensive perimeter around the dock; demolition squads would destroy carefully selected installations; and protection squads would give them security from German attack. A 90-minute window of time was allocated to land the assault troops, carry out all planned demolitions, and then depart aboard the vessels that had landed them ashore before the Germans reacted in strength to the raid. To fit them for this highly specialized task the demolition squads underwent an intensive period of instruction in blowing up port installations in dockyards in the UK.

The small British naval flotilla detailed for Operation *Chariot*, commanded by Cdr Robert Ryder, consisted of two destroyers (HMS *Tynedale* and HMS *Atherstone*) as escorts; HMS *Campbeltown* (loaded with 9,600 lb. of high explosive contained in depth charges and packed full of assault, protection and demolition Commando troops); a motor gun boat (MGB 314); a specially modified motor torpedo boat (MTB 74); and 16 motor launches (MLs) carrying other parties of Commandos. It left Falmouth on 26 March and took a circuitous route deep into the Bay of Biscay ostensibly on a long-range anti-submarine sweep into the bay. Unfortunately it did not succeed in escaping German attention: a U-Boat (U-593) sighted the destroyers and MLs. Although the submarine quickly lost contact, the whole plan was briefly thrown into doubt. Displaying considerable moral courage, the force commander decided to press on, and not long after it ran into a small group of French trawlers. It sank two, after removing their crews, and the flotilla pressed on towards St Nazaire. As it approached the French coast the two escorting destroyers moved away as planned to patrol offshore. A submarine – HMS *Sturgeon* – standing off the coast acted as a valuable navigational beacon for the assault flotilla as it made its final approach, assumed an attack formation, and began its carefully

Cdr Robert Ryder VC, Naval Force Commander for Operation *Chariot*. (HU 1916)

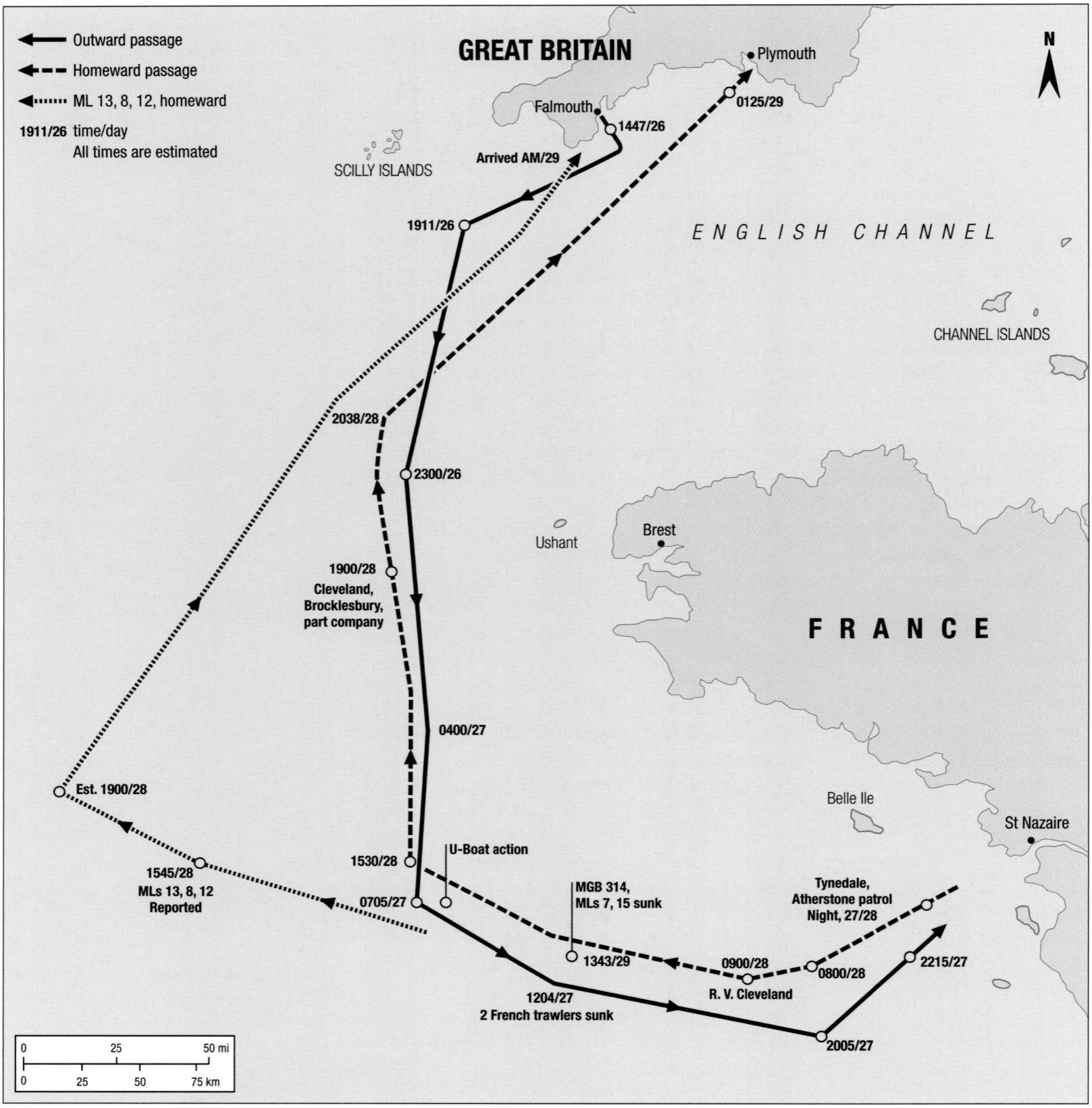
Outward passage
Homeward passage
ML 13, 8, 12, homeward
1911/26 time/day
All times are estimated
GREAT BRITAIN
Plymouth
Falmouth
1447/26
0125/29
SCILLY ISLANDS
Arrived AM/29
1911/26
ENGLISH CHANNEL
CHANNEL ISLANDS
2038/28
2300/26
Ushant
Brest
1900/28
Cleveland, Brocklesbury, part company
FRANCE
0400/27
Est. 1900/28
Belle Ile
St Nazaire
U-Boat action
1530/28
1545/28
MLs 13, 8, 12
Reported
0705/27
MGB 314,
MLs 7, 15 sunk
Tynedale,
Atherstone patrol
Night, 27/28
1343/29
0900/28
0800/28
2215/27
R. V. Cleveland
1204/27
2 French trawlers sunk
2005/27
0 25 50 mi
0 25 50 75 km
N

The outward and homeward routes taken by the St Nazaire raiding force.

charted journey through the mud flats and shoals at the entrance to the River Loire. At 1200 hours RAF Bomber Command launched its diversionary raid on St Nazaire, although low cloud and an overcast sky meant the aircraft did not bomb the port as intended for fear of killing French civilians. Instead, aircraft circled overhead and dropped the occasional bomb in the vicinity of the port to hold German attention.

The flotilla quickly entered the estuary of the River Loire on the night of 27/28 March, led by Newman and Ryder aboard MGB 314; two motor launches armed with torpedoes; and then HMS *Campbeltown*, commanded by Lt Cdr Stephen Beattie and loaded with Maj Bill Copland, 2i/c No. 2 Commando, two assault parties, five demolition parties and a 3in. mortar group. On either flank and to the rear were the Fairmile MLs carrying the remaining Commandos with MTB 74 coming up the rear. As planned, the high tide allowed the lightened

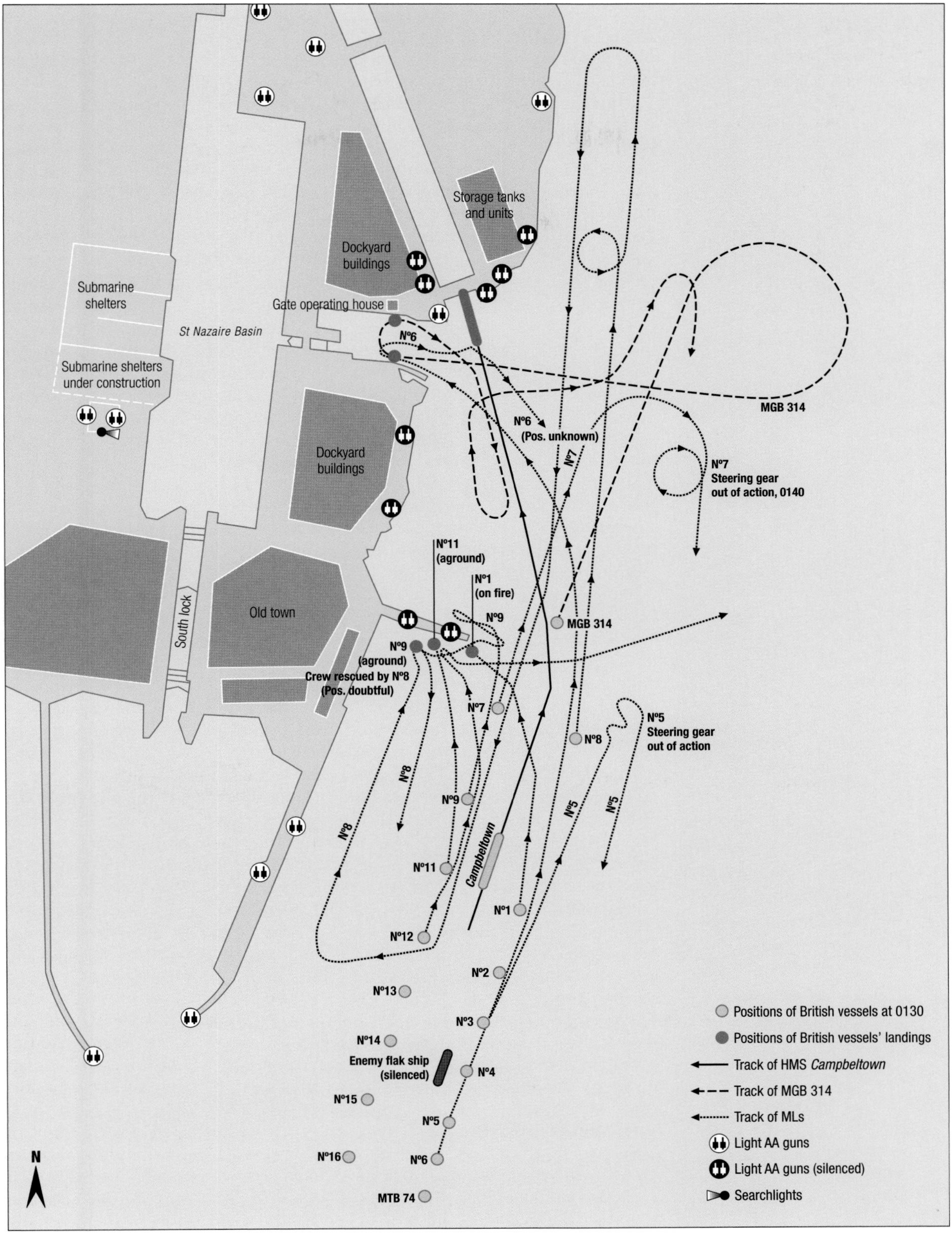
Storage tanks and units
Dockyard buildings
Submarine shelters
Gate operating house
St Nazaire Basin
Submarine shelters under construction
Nº6
MGB 314
Nº6 (Pos. unknown)
Dockyard buildings
Nº7
Nº7 Steering gear out of action, 0140
Nº11 (aground)
Nº1 (on fire)
South lock
Old town
Nº9
MGB 314
Nº9 (aground)
Crew rescued by Nº8 (Pos. doubtful)
Nº7
Nº5 Steering gear out of action
Nº8
Nº8
Nº9
Nº5
Nº5
Nº8
Campbeltown
Nº11
Nº1
Nº12
Nº2
Nº13
Nº3
Nº14
Enemy flak ship (silenced)
Nº4
Nº15
Nº5
Nº16
Nº6
MTB 74
N
Positions of British vessels at 0130
Positions of British vessels' landings
Track of HMS Campbeltown
Track of MGB 314
Track of MLs
Light AA guns
Light AA guns (silenced)
Searchlights

The objectives and progress of the Commando teams at St Nazaire, 0130–0200 hours, 28 March.

HMS *Campbeltown* to largely avoid using the Charpentier Channel and cross several shoals, although it grounded on two occasions. The deception plan in place for Operation *Chariot*, moreover, lived up to expectations, allowing the flotilla to pass the main coastal batteries without interference.

Unfortunately the heavily disguised HMS *Campbeltown* and accompanying small craft were identified as hostile after they had proceeded some distance down the long estuary of the River Loire in the early hours of 28 March. Indeed, instead of diverting attention the air raids by RAF Bomber Command had done the opposite by putting the German defences on alert. Illuminated by searchlights the game was soon up for HMS *Campbeltown* and the flotilla. Despite further attempts to confuse the defenders using captured codebooks and the efforts of a German-speaking petty officer that bought a few minutes, at 0128 hours the Germans finally identified the ship as hostile and opened fire while the assault force was still six minutes out from the objective. Although German fire was initially confused and desultory, it quickly increased in intensity as heavier weapons were brought to bear on the fast-moving warships. Heavy losses were immediately inflicted upon the escorting wooden Fairmile MLs and aboard ship by German coastal defences and anti-aircraft guns, which raked them as they increased to full speed ahead. Return fire was immediately opened by the flotilla, suppressing some of the German batteries, but casualties aboard all the ships quickly mounted. At 0134 hours the badly damaged HMS *Campbeltown* successfully rammed the dock gates going at a speed of 20 knots, achieving the primary objective of the raid before the Commandos had even landed. A delayed action fuse was immediately set and further demolition charges scuttled the ship in place half on the dock gate and half in the water.

The surviving Commando assault and demolition parties aboard – fewer than 100 men after earlier casualties inflicted on the run into the port – quickly disembarked from the warship. Under heavy German fire, the former quickly tackled German gun positions, while the latter laid explosive charges on their designated targets, including the pumping station, winding station and the other dry dock gate. Confusion reigned in the area with German tracer from surviving gun positions criss-crossing the dockyard area and night sky. Behind them Lt Col Newman and his command group quickly disembarked and coincidentally took up position nearby in a German dockyard HQ.

The parties of Commandos tasked with disembarking at the Old Mole and Old Entrance fared far worse than those on the destroyer, with the vulnerable MLs carrying them being savaged by devastating German defensive fire long before they arrived. Many failed to reach their objective and only a handful of men made it ashore from their sinking craft. Only 20 of the intended 70 Commandos, for example, from one ML got ashore at the Old Mole. Those Commandos who landed were too few in number to achieve the result intended; as a result, many carefully selected targets were left untouched, and most importantly the disembarkation point around the Old Mole was left in enemy hands.

The successes achieved by the Commandos landed near HMS *Campbeltown* proved short-lived and limited in extent. As the surprised German defences – comprising in total over 5,000 soldiers and sailors – slowly reacted, the surviving Commandos on completion of their assigned tasks withdrew to where MLs would pick them up for the return voyage. Many men found their only means of escape already destroyed, with the river littered with dead bodies, floating wreckage and blazing MLs drifting amongst pools of burning oil. The few vessels that had survived had had little alternative but to withdraw. An overland escape from the German noose tightening around the port was now the only alternative to capture.

The remaining Commandos – some 50–70 men, many of whom were wounded – led by Lt Col Newman attempted to fight their way out of the dock area, through the Old Town and into the open country that lay beyond to make good their escape. This breakout met heavy German resistance and as daylight broke the survivors split into smaller and smaller groups that had little alternative other than going to ground in alleys, sheds and back gardens in the Old Town. The Germans quickly sealed off the area, however, before beginning a systematic search for survivors. Although a few Commandos successfully evaded capture and escaped through the German cordon thrown around St Nazaire across country, the remainder, many of whom were wounded, surrendered as soon as it became daylight to German patrols or at checkpoints. The survivors of the Commando assault force and RN prisoners going into German captivity for the rest of the war, however, had the satisfaction of seeing the final result of the raid. At 1030 hours the following day the four tons of depth charges aboard HMS *Campbeltown* detonated (long after intended), killing an estimated 400 German sightseers inspecting the damage to the dock, and effectively wrecking the installation for the rest of the war. To compound the Germans' confusion, torpedoes fired from MTB 74, fitted with delayed action fuses, later detonated, damaging the outer caisson of the Old Entrance, although they failed to destroy it.

The 'greatest raid of all' was declared an immediate success by the British high command and the ensuing publicity greeted with enthusiasm by the British public. The Normandie dry dock remained out of action for the rest of World War II, effectively preventing the Germans deploying capital ships on the Atlantic coast of France. Further German resources were devoted to the defence of the French seaboard. The cost, however, had been heavy, with only the two supporting destroyers, a handful of MLs and MGB 314 returning across the English Channel to safety. Out of a total of 611 men who had begun the attack 169 were killed, including 64 Commandos and 105 Royal Navy personnel. Only 40 percent of the force returned home, with the remaining survivors entering German captivity. 83 decorations for gallantry were awarded, including five Victoria Crosses. A further 51 men were Mentioned in Despatches. A further five Commandos evaded capture, and made their way out of France and into Spain.

Operation *Infatuate*: the 1944 assault on Walcheren

The November 1944 assault on the island of Walcheren, lying at the mouth of the estuary of the River Scheldt in Holland, was the last major opposed amphibious operation mounted by the Commandos in North-West Europe during World War II. 4th Special Service Brigade, consisting of Nos. 41, 47 and 48 (RM) Commandos and No. 4 Commando, under the command of Brig Bernard 'Jumbo' Leicester, was chosen to capture this strategic island, whose powerful coastal guns dominated the mouth of the Scheldt and the approach to Antwerp lying 25 miles up-river. This large port had to be kept operational in order to supply Allied forces operating in Europe.

Walcheren Island was heavily defended by elements of the German 15th Army, garrisoned by approximately 10,000 low-grade troops belonging primarily to the static 70th Infantry Division commanded by Generalleutnant Wilhelm Daser. Although dubbed the 'White Bread Division' because most of its troops had stomach complaints or wounds of some sort or other, its ranks contained a fair proportion of combat veterans. Most of these troops occupied an impressive array of fixed concrete defences – part of the so-called Atlantic Wall – protected along the shoreline by extensive minefields and beach obstacles intended to defeat an amphibious landing. The coastal batteries dominating the approaches to the island were equipped with a formidable array of anti-aircraft and large-calibre (150mm or greater) coastal defence guns, located on a rim of high sand dunes and massive dykes surrounding

Walcheren. These formidable coastal batteries were manned by naval troops, commanded by Seekommandant Kapitain zur See Frank Aschman, whose command was divided into a Marine Artillerie Abteilung manning the guns and Flak Abteilung 810, distributed around the island. The latter's anti-aircraft guns could be used in both an air and ground role.

The highly ambitious plan for Operation *Infatuate* consisted of an opposed amphibious landing by three Commandos, reinforced by No. 4 (Belgian) and No. 5 (Norwegian) Troops of No. 10 (Inter-Allied) Commando, at Westkappelle on the western side of the island. No. 41 (RM) Commando would clear this small town and then advance northwards along the dyke, rolling up the German defences, while No. 47 (RM) Commando and No. 48 (RM) Commando advanced southwards towards Flushing, clearing successive coastal forts built in a belt of high dunes. Simultaneously No. 4 Commando, commanded by Lt Col Dawson, with the assistance of No. 1 and 8 (French) Troops of No. 10 (IA) Commando, would cross by landing craft from Breskens and launch an assault on Flushing from the southern side of the island, with 155th Infantry Brigade (part of 52nd Division) following in support. The main body of 52nd Lowland Division and 2nd Canadian Division, meanwhile, would attack along the north bank of the river and try to cross the causeway onto the island, although it quickly became apparent the mudflats on either side were completely impassable leaving them the only option of seizing the causeway.

4th Special Service Brigade faced making another opposed frontal amphibious assault against a heavily defended shoreline bristling with coastal batteries, minefields and beach obstacles. Intensive training was undertaken near Ostend during October, using captured German gun emplacements, fortifications and blockhouses in the area similar to those on Walcheren, to prepare its troops and instruct them in how to overcome German coastal fortifications. These veterans of the D-Day assault received refresher training in the technique of mounting an amphibious assault and were introduced to new equipment. Instead of using vulnerable Landing Craft Infantry, armoured Weasel and Buffalo tracked amphibious vehicles (LVTs) were employed by the assault troops to carry them ashore. A considerable amount of time was devoted to familiarization with these new vehicles, of which the Commandos had little experience. A succession of attacks by RAF Bomber Command, meanwhile, softened up the defences of Walcheren by breaching the dykes that ringed the island at Westkappelle, Veere and on either side of Flushing, and flooded the low-lying central area. This had the effect of turning the central area into a large lagoon and thereby limiting the Germans' freedom of manoeuvre to areas above water level, and denying them use of some defensive positions. It also meant all attacks had to be down the narrow coastal strip on an easily predicted axis of advance precluding surprise and outflanking attacks. A vast panoply of weapons was placed in support of the assault landing and ensuing fighting, including RAF Typhoon fighter-bombers, naval gunfire support from the 15in.-gun battleship HMS *Warspite*, and the monitors HMS *Roberts* and *Erebus*; a specialized Support Squadron 'Eastern Flank', consisting of

4th Special Service Brigade order of battle, Walcheren, November 1944

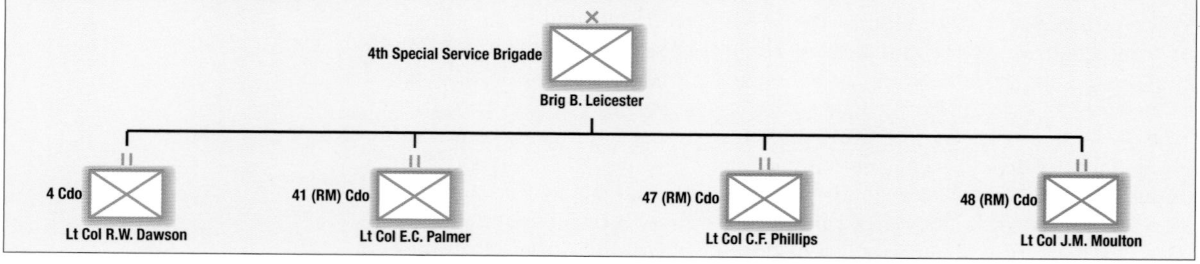
4th Special Service Brigade
Brig B. Leicester
4 Cdo
Lt Col R.W. Dawson
41 (RM) Cdo
Lt Col E.C. Palmer
47 (RM) Cdo
Lt Col C.F. Phillips
48 (RM) Cdo
Lt Col J.M. Moulton

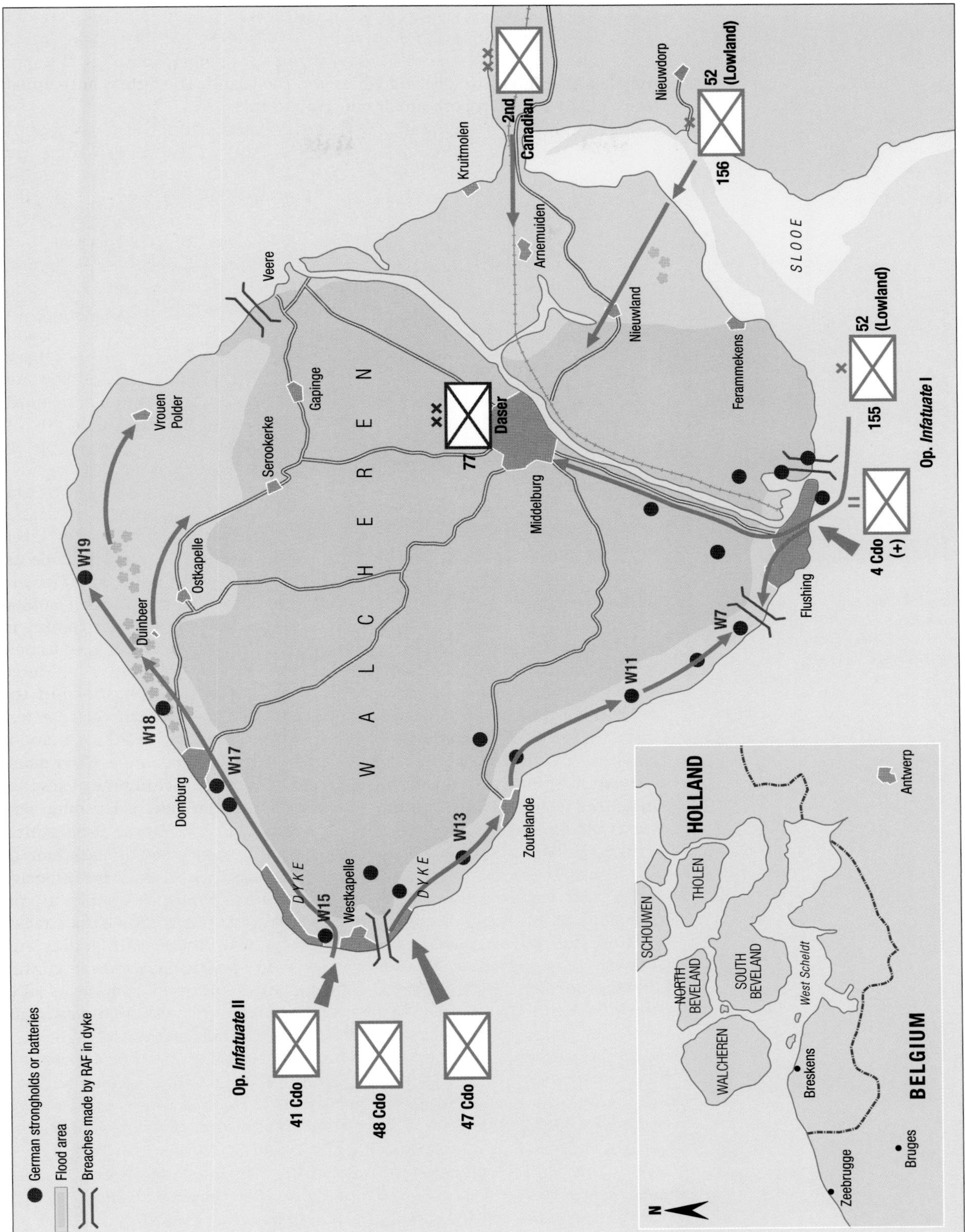
German strongholds or batteries
Flood area
Breaches made by RAF in dyke
Op. Infatuate II
41 Cdo
48 Cdo
47 Cdo
W15
Westkapelle
DYKE
DYKE
W13
Zoutelande
Domburg
W17
W18
Duinbeer
W19
Ostkapelle
Vrouen Polder
Serookerke
Gapinge
Veere
W A L C H E R E N
77
Daser
Middelburg
W11
W7
Flushing
4 Cdo (+)
Op. Infatuate I
155
52 (Lowland)
Ferammekens
Nieuwland
Arnemuiden
Kruitmolen
2nd Canadian
156
52 (Lowland)
Nieuwdorp
SLOOE
HOLLAND
SCHOUWEN
THOLEN
NORTH BEVELAND
SOUTH BEVELAND
WALCHEREN
West Scheldt
Breskens
BELGIUM
Antwerp
Zeebrugge
Bruges
N

Operation *Infatuate I* and *II*, Walcheren, 1944. The inset map shows the location of the Scheldt estuary.

Buffaloes and Weasels operating in support of 41 (RM) Commando at Westkapelle, Walcheren, 1 November 1944. (B11646)

Landing Craft Gun, Landing Craft Support, Landing Craft Flak and Landing Craft Rocket would also provide close-in support. Massed British and Canadian artillery batteries in the Breskens area and specialist tanks from 79th Armoured Division took part in the assault too.

Operation *Infatuate* began soon after the Germans occupying the Breskens pocket had been eliminated and North and South Beveland had been cleared of enemy troops. The attack on Flushing – Operation *Infatuate I* – by No. 4 Commando, commanded by Lt Col Dawson, began well on 1 November, although RAF support was curtailed by poor weather over the airfields. A bridgehead was secured with minimal casualties near the town, after which its men cleared a succession of German strongpoints as the leading battalion of 155th Infantry Brigade came ashore in support. By 1600 most objectives had been secured, leaving only a handful remaining to be cleared the following day.

The main assault at Westkappelle – Operation *Infatuate II* – made by the main body of 4th Special Service Brigade at 0945 hours on 1 November, fared less well, and due to poor weather in the UK was denied air support. The German coast guns that had survived previous heavy bombardments and bombing opened effective fire upon the supporting vessels and LTVs as they approached either side of the breach near Westkappelle. Many landing craft were sunk and others damaged in an unequal duel carried out between the support squadron and the German defences that lasted most of the day. No. 41 (RM) Commando, commanded by Lt Col E.C. Palmer, landed as planned and with tank support cleared Westkappelle by 1115 hours before advancing northwards along the narrow dyke. It attacked and successfully cleared several German defensive positions, including W15 armed with British 4.7in. guns captured in 1940. Domburg was occupied by 1815 hours, with the Germans concentrated in a wooded area to the north. At 1010 the assault wave of No. 48 (RM) Commando, led by Lt Col J.L. Moulton, landed south of the breach, secured a bridgehead, and advanced on Zoutelande, two miles to the south, along a narrow strip of high ground (only 150 yards wide) running between the sea and flooded area of the island. As one officer described:

> Along this rim the Marines had to fight their way, with no room to manoeuvre – just a grim slog through the deep, loose sand dune against an enemy well protected by his solid concrete.[24]

No. 48 (RM) Commando, after making initially good progress, however, was held up by a heavily defended German coastal battery (W13), which was taken and silenced by the end of the day only after an intensive bombardment and a carefully concerted attack. At a cost of seven killed and 80 wounded, the Commando had secured the southern flank of the bridgehead.

The following day – 2 November – the village of Zoutelande unexpectedly fell to the advancing 48 (RM) Commando, as the Germans retreated to regroup, after which No. 47 (RM) Commando, commanded by Lt Col C.F. Phillips, took over the lead during the afternoon. A strongly fortified coastal battery, however, located above Dishoek and dubbed W11, held up the advance; its four undamaged 150mm guns kept up fire on the initial landing beach. Heavy fighting occurred before the battery was silenced, but in the process No. 47 (RM) Commando lost five troop leaders and a number of other senior officers and NCOs, as well as 60 ORs killed or wounded. As a result it withdrew to regroup away from the main position. A German counterattack failed to retake the strongpoint that night, although it came close to overrunning the Commandos. The following day W11 was finally secured. No. 47 (RM) Commando then pushed on southwards, secured W4 Battery and met elements of No. 4 Commando at the gap in the dyke near Flushing. The latter and the 4th and 5th Battalion KOSB had cleared Flushing after heavy fighting on D+1.

No. 41 (RM) Commando and two attached troops of No. 10 (IA) Commando reached the northern side of Domburg on the morning of D+1, where strong German resistance was encountered. Four fighting troops – two each from No. 41 (RM) Command and No. 10 (IA) Commando – were left behind, supported by the 1st Lothians' remaining tanks, while the main body of No. 41 Commando was suddenly transferred southwards on 2 November to assist No. 47 (RM) Commando when it was held up by a strong German defensive position. On 3 November it was ferried over the gap at Westkappelle and by evening had assembled at Zoutelande where it was discovered that Battery W11 had already fallen to No. 47 (RM) and No. 48 (RM) Commando. Nos. 4, 47 (RM) and 48 (RM) Commandos concentrated in Zoutelande where a two-day pause occurred while supply difficulties (caused by poor weather that prevented further landings at Westkappelle) were sorted out. Both No. 4 and No. 47 (RM) Commandos continued northwards through a scene of devastation in support of No. 41 (RM) Commando to clear the remaining German centre of resistance north-west of Domburg.

A lunch group consisting of Brig B.W. 'Jumbo' Leicester and officers of 41 (Royal Marine) Commando and Maj G. Franks, 2i/c 10 (IA) Commando at Westkapelle, November 1944. (B11640)

Meanwhile 155th Infantry Brigade, after clearing Flushing of remaining German pockets of resistance, advanced down the line of the canal towards Middleburg, using Buffalo LVTs to assist in flooded areas. No opposition was encountered when it entered the town on 6 November and large numbers of Germans eagerly surrendered, including the GOC 70th Division.

No. 41 (RM) Commando retraced its steps and was back in position at Domburg by noon on 4 November, with further operations planned to deal with German troops concentrated north-west of the village. On 5 November the advance was delayed until 1500 hours, however, to ensure air support was available for the attack on W18. This commanding anti-aircraft position was taken, but further supply difficulties delayed a later advance. The following day the advance continued along the coast, although hampered by minefields and limited German resistance. On 8 November an early morning attack on W19 proved immediately successful, with large numbers of German prisoners being taken. The same day, the last remaining battery was assaulted by No. 41 (RM) Commando, while No. 4 Commando cleared the Overduin Woods and then pushed eastwards towards Vrouwenpolder opposite North Beveland. A heavy bombardment from supporting artillery and the brigade mortars of each Commando had a significant effect, and a steady flow of prisoners was taken by the advancing troops. Organized German resistance steadily slackened and at 0815 hours on 9 November a deputation reached No. 4 Commando's HQ asking to formally surrender all remaining troops in the area. Following a brief negotiation with the German commander in Vrouwenpoler, a cease-fire was ordered, bringing the bloody battle for Walcheren to an end. It had been a tough fight hampered by poor weather that on occasion limited the amount of support received by the Commandos. As one eyewitness recorded:

> The advance had been hard. The weather had broken up from the third day, with a tempestuous wind blowing. The ground was strewn with mines and progress had been slow, and deadly ... 40,000 Germans had been put out of action by this operation.
>
> After a short time, we had left the island, and on our arrival at Ostend, we presented the classic sight of soldiers returning from the front. Our clothes stiffened by dry mud which was glued to them, we bent under the load of our rucksacks filled with many memories ...

Troops of 1st Commando Brigade man two Vickers medium machine guns in the shattered outskirts of Wesel during the Rhine crossing, 24–31 March 1945. (BU 2329)

Our eyelids were reddened through lack of sleep and more than one chin sported a hairy beard. In spite of our tiredness, we had the feeling of having accomplished something.[25]

The end of Operation *Infatuate* came with the surrender of the remainder of the German garrison. Although ultimately successful, it had been a stern test of the Commandos. The opposed amphibious assault, the strength of the German fixed defences and the close nature of the ensuing fighting along the rim of the island had meant casualties were heavy. By the end of the fighting No. 4 Commando Brigade had lost 103 killed, 325 wounded and 68 missing during eight days' intensive fighting. By the end of the month, after the Scheldt estuary and port facilities had been swept of mines, the Port of Antwerp opened for traffic. It was not a moment too soon, moreover, with the German Ardennes offensive the following month placing a massive strain on the entire Allied logistical structure in North-West Europe.

The battle for Hill 170: 3rd Commando Brigade in Arakan, February 1945

3rd Special Service Brigade, commanded by Brig W.I. Nonweiler, had gone aboard ship and was despatched to join South-East Asia Command soon after its formation. It consisted of No. 1, No. 5, No. 42 (RM) and No. 44 (RM) Commandos, with the Dutch Troop of No. 10 (IA) temporarily under command. However, its commander quickly discovered that there was little prospect of employing it in an amphibious role, since few landing craft were available due to the demands of other theatres of war. Following acclimatization and intensive jungle training in India Command, it received its baptism of fire and gained hard-won practical experience of the jungle and the Japanese in Arakan in March 1944. Following the decisive defeat of the Japanese HA-GO offensive it took part in a limited counteroffensive to clear the heavily contested Maungdaw–Buthidaung road. As part of XV Indian Corps the Commandos quickly discovered that jungle fighting was very different from that fought in Europe, where they were committed to battle primarily in an infantry role. As one officer later wrote: 'This is a very different type of war and you are fighting against a genuine fanatic who fires and expects no quarter.' A series of small-scale operations, however, were also carried out by elements of the brigade along the shore of Arakan. Early in April elements of the 3rd Special Service Brigade were transferred to Assam, where, under appalling monsoon conditions of intense heat, high humidity and torrential rainfall, they blocked a possible Japanese advance along the Silchar Track from the Imphal Plain. Following the defeat of the so-called Japanese 'March on Delhi' in July 1944, they were withdrawn into reserve once again in India Command.

The renamed 3rd Commando Brigade, now commanded by Brig Campbell Hardy, rejoined XV Indian Corps in December 1944 as it resumed the offensive down the Arakan coast aimed at the capture of Rangoon. A series of large- and small-scale amphibious assaults began down the jungle and mangrove swamp-fringed coastline, fully exploiting Allied command of the sea and at last the availability of assault shipping. These assaults were intended to outflank the Japanese 28th Army, which was slowly withdrawing southwards to join hands with the rest of Burma Area Army facing the advancing British 14th Army in central Burma.

The vital Akyab Island, having a small port and several badly needed airfields, formed the first objective for XV Indian Corps, with 3rd Commando Brigade tasked with mounting an assault landing on 3 January 1945 followed by 26th Indian Division. At the last minute a light aircraft manned by No. 656 (AOP) Squadron, however, discovered by landing on the deserted airfield that the Japanese had already decamped and when the Commandos landed

3rd Commando Brigade order of battle, Arakan, January–February 1945

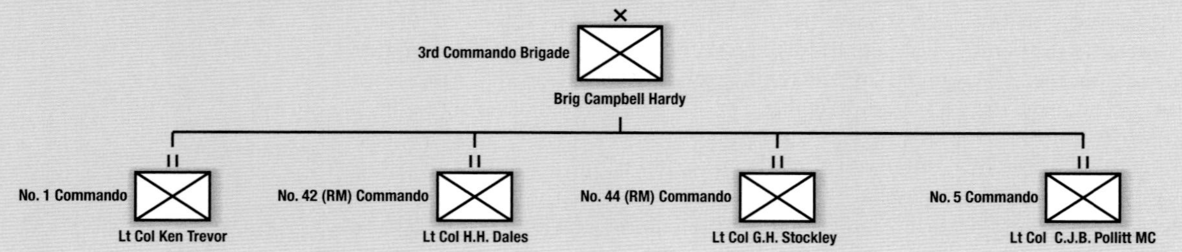
3rd Commando Brigade
Brig Campbell Hardy
No. 1 Commando
Lt Col Ken Trevor
No. 42 (RM) Commando
Lt Col H.H. Dales
No. 44 (RM) Commando
Lt Col G.H. Stockley
No. 5 Commando
Lt Col C.J.B. Pollitt MC

no opposition was encountered. A series of reconnaissance patrols in LCAs in the surrounding coastal inlets (chaungs) gave Commandos valuable further experience.

Following the bloodless capture of Akyab Island, the Commandos spearheaded an assault on the nearby Myebon peninsula, located 30 miles to the south-east of Akyab, intended to deny 28th Army the use of an important concentration area and two waterways (the Kyatsin River and Daingbon Chaung) it commanded. On 12 January No. 42 (RM) Commando made the first successful landing, although deep mud meant further landings were switched to another beach. Even so, it quickly seized its objectives and No. 5 Commando passed through. Myebon Village was captured the following day and with tank support a number of defended hill features were cleared of the enemy. The advance brigade of 25th Indian Division landed on 18 January, took over the lead from the Commandos, and cleared the rest of the peninsula, although the Japanese sealed off its base and occupied a series of strongpoints that made further progress impossible.

The only escape route remaining to the Japanese 54th Division, under heavy pressure from West African troops advancing southwards down the Kaladan Valley, was now the Myohaung–Tamandu road. An overland advance to cut this road at Kangaw Village, a supply point and minor naval base, where the only road suitable for motor vehicles left the plains and entered the jungle-covered hills, was clearly extremely difficult, since it involved crossing three watercourses that offered the Japanese ideal defensive positions. A surprise amphibious landing was immediately planned by the GOC XV Indian Corps employing a deep, 27-mile-long twisting, narrow coastal inlet running through thick mangrove swamps – the Daingbon Chaung – as an indirect line of approach. The aim was to outflank the Myebon peninsula and cut the lines of communication of Japanese troops fighting further north. It would employ a mixture of minesweepers, RIN sloops, landing craft, lighters and other assorted river craft to carry the assault troops, as well as a battery of 25-pounder guns aboard large self-propelled barges to provide immediate artillery support.

The leading elements of 3rd Commando Brigade landed two miles south-west of Kangaw at 1300 hours on 22 January, under the cover of a smokescreen. This initial landing, deliberately made without ground or air support to avoid alerting the Japanese in the area, achieved complete surprise. Going was extremely difficult, however, for the advancing troops of No. 1 Commando, commanded by Lt Col Ken Trevor, as they moved out of the bridgehead established between two chaungs. As Peter Young writes:

> The landing was through mangrove swamp; the paddy for ¾ mile, leading up to 170 was swamped by the spring tides. Even the bunds didn't make proper footpaths being broken in many places. No tanks could be got ashore – or guns – the first few days, but we had air support, mediums for the Myebon area and a lighter battery, a sloop. MLs and LCs guarded the chaung L. of C. [Lines of Communication][26]

No. 1 Commando quickly occupied a 700-yard-long, 300-yard-wide and 100ft-high wooded ridge – Hill 170 (codenamed *Brighton*) – lying between the chaung and Kabaw Village. While No. 42 (RM) Commando established a bridgehead between two chaungs dubbed the Thames and Mersey, No. 5 Commando moved forward in support of No. 1 Commando, and next morning the complete hill feature was in British hands. No. 44 (RM) Commando secured Milford on the 22nd and the next morning secured Pinner as it advanced on Kangaw, having only encountered light Japanese resistance.

Unsurprisingly the Japanese quickly reacted to this serious new threat and hurriedly redeployed infantry and artillery to counterattack 3rd Commando Brigade. On the night of 23/24 January the Japanese counterattacked Pinner and effective artillery fire pounded the defences on Hill 170. This shelling, unprecedented in intensity for the theatre of war, continued for the next four days. As planned, 51st Indian Infantry Brigade, accompanied by a troop of Sherman V tanks of the 19th Lancers, landed on 26 January and gradually took over the forward positions established by the Commandos on hilltops overlooking the main road. On 28/29 January, 51st Indian Infantry Brigade attacked Kangaw and both Perth and Melrose dominating the road to the east of it, but only partially achieved its objectives as Japanese opposition hardened. Even so Kangaw Village was captured and positions occupied from which the road could be covered by machine guns and observed artillery fire by day, while ambushes made it impassable to Japanese units during the hours of darkness.

The Commandos were preparing to withdraw, as part of a planned relief, on 30 January when the newly arrived Japanese Mattsu Detachment struck back in what quickly became the most desperate and bitter fighting of the Third Arakan campaign. At dawn on 31 January a reinforced Japanese infantry battalion, part of the 154th Regiment, launched a fierce surprise attack on Hill 170 under cover of intense MG fire and a heavy artillery bombardment, occupied by No. 1 and No. 42 (RM) Commando with a troop of the 19th Indian Lancers in support. A tank laager at the foot of the northern end of the hill was attacked by a party of Japanese assault engineers early in the morning, who successfully destroyed a Sherman V and other vehicles before being killed to a man. Furious attacks and counterattacks continued throughout the day with the northern end of the feature bearing the brunt. No. 4 Troop of No. 1 Command, occupying a semi-detached hillock at the northern end of Hill 170, came under heavy sustained pressure and during its defence Lt George Knowland won a posthumous Victoria Cross during a series of counterattacks to maintain his forward positions. No. 1 and No. 42 Commandos held firm or else fiercely counterattacked as the day progressed to cut off enemy lodgements, albeit at heavy cost from enemy MG and artillery fire. On occasion, fierce hand-to-hand fighting raged about the defences. Enormous

Commandos and Sherman tanks press home a counterattack near Hill 170, Arakan, January 1945. (IND 4357)

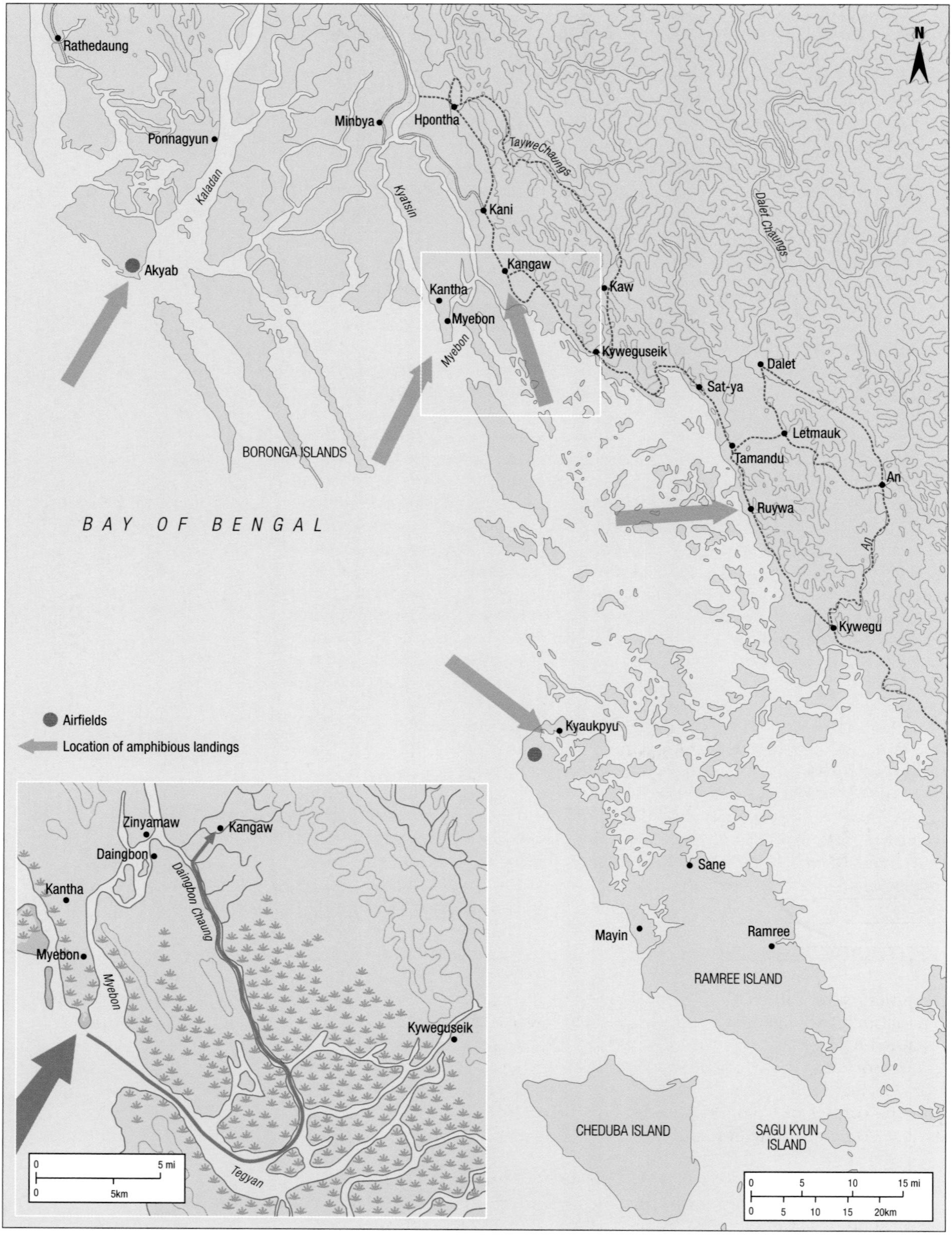
Rathedaung
Minbya
Hpontha
Ponnagyun
Kaladan
TayweChaungs
Kyatsin
Kani
Dalet Chaungs
Akyab
Kangaw
Kaw
Kantha
Myebon
Myebon
Kyweguseik
Dalet
Sat-ya
Letmauk
BORONGA ISLANDS
Tamandu
An
Ruywa
BAY OF BENGAL
An
Kywegu
Airfields
Location of amphibious landings
Kyaukpyu
Zinyamaw
Kangaw
Daingbon
Daingbon Chaung
Kantha
Sane
Myebon
Myebon
Mayin
Ramree
RAMREE ISLAND
Kyweguseik
CHEDUBA ISLAND
SAGU KYUN ISLAND
Tegyan
0 5 mi
0 5km
0 5 10 15 mi
0 5 10 15 20km

 The amphibious landings in South Arakan and central Burma, and the approach to Kangaw.

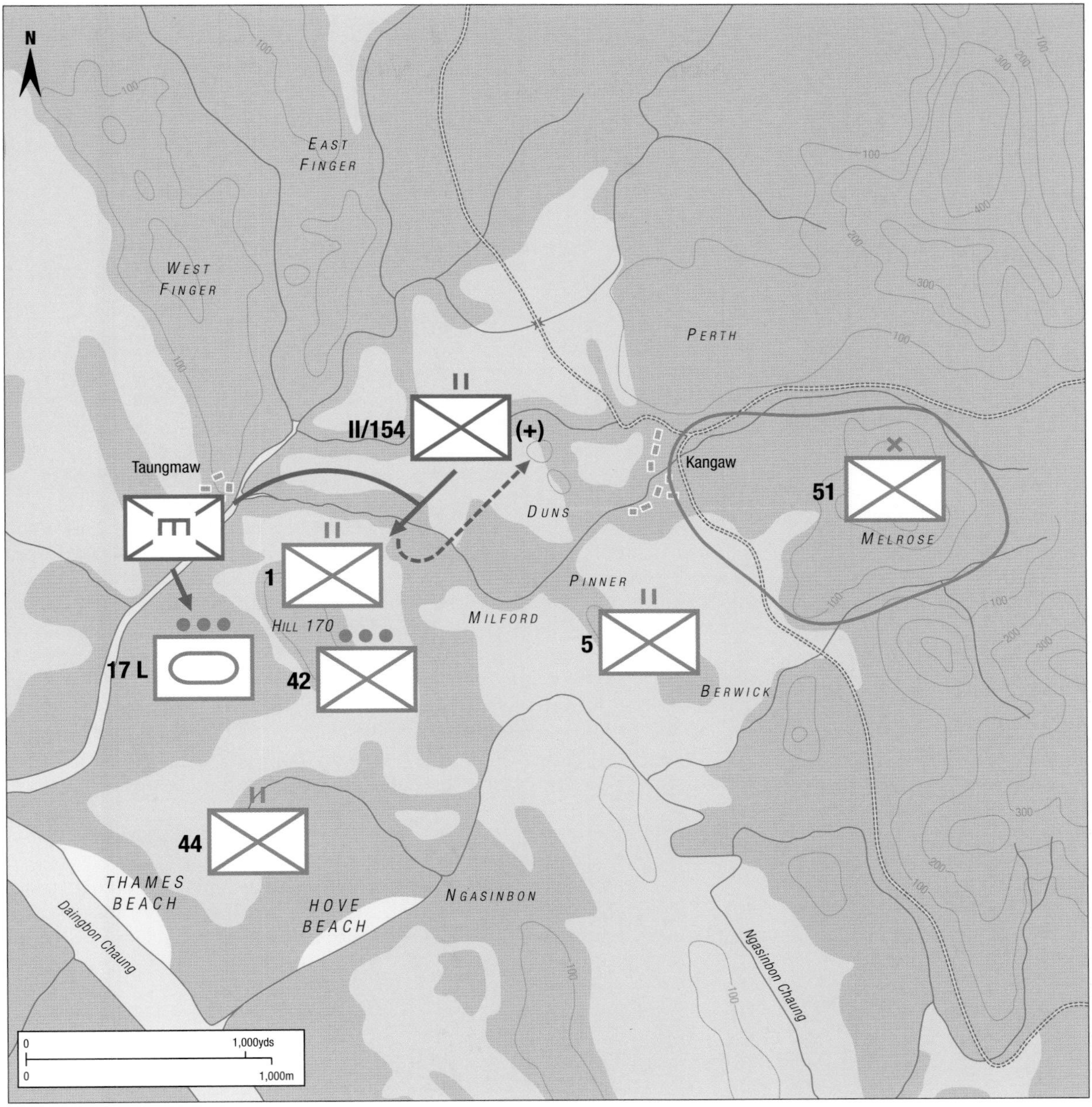
N
East Finger
West Finger
Perth
II/154
(+)
Taungmaw
Kangaw
51
Duns
Melrose
1
Pinner
17 L
Hill 170
Milford
5
42
Berwick
44
Thames Beach
Hove Beach
Ngasinbon
Daingbon Chaung
Ngasinbon Chaung
0
1,000yds
1,000m

The fighting around Hill 170, Arakan.

casualties were inflicted on the enemy, who fought with considerable 'fanaticism'. The Japanese attacks had finally ceased by 1700 hours, having sustained heavy casualties and by next morning the Commandos had cleared and consolidated the position. By the morning of 1 February the fighting was over, leaving the hillside littered with over 340 Japanese dead intermingled with the corpses of Commandos who had died after desperate hand-to-hand combat. As Peter Young described:

> Jap dead were inter-locked with our own in proportion of at least 3 to 1. The back slopes of the hill were thick with the victims of our 25 pdrs and 3in. mortars which respectively fired at positions 100 and 40 yds ahead of our own troops! It was a real epic. I never saw dead so thick … I am convinced that no British troops ever fought better than ours on that day.

The heroic defence of Hill 170 by 3rd Commando Brigade effectively decided the fate of the Japanese 28th Army in Arakan. The importance of seizing this hill feature had clearly been identified by the enemy. Without it the rest of 3rd Commando Brigade and 51st Indian Infantry Brigade would have been cut off from the beachhead, and the whole landing operation at Kangaw would have failed in its objective of cutting off the escape of the Japanese 54th Division. This largely accounted for the ferocity of the fanatical attacks. To quote one officer:

> The Japanese had attacked with a fanatical, brutish courage which lacked subtlety and made little use of manoeuvre. But the man who had put them in to attack Hill 170 had put his finger unerringly on the key to the whole position.[28]

Further enemy attacks continued around Myebon, but the Japanese high command soon realized that further landings on the coast, further advances by 25th Indian Division inland from the Myebon peninsula, and advances by 82nd (West African) Division from the north made their position untenable. Consequently, a general withdrawal from the area was ordered to avoid complete destruction. Enemy resistance at Kangaw rapidly diminished and by 18 February 25th Indian Division had finished mopping up the area.

The defence of Hill 170 had been a stern test of the courage, endurance and fighting qualities of 3rd Commando Brigade, which was reflected in the award of a Victoria Cross, a third DSO to Brig Campbell-Hardy and a DSO to Lt Col Ken Trevor. Both officers and men were heaped with praise by senior British commanders and were the subject of considerable publicity. In a Special Order of the Day to 3rd Commando Brigade, Lt Gen Sir Philip Christison, commander of XV Corps, concluded: 'The Battle of Kangaw has been the decisive battle of the whole Arakan campaign, and that it was won was very largely due to your magnificent defence of Hill 170.' Similarly Maj Gen N. Wood, GOC 25th Indian Division, whose men had worked in close cooperation with Commandos throughout the Third Arakan campaign, wrote:

> I wish, on behalf of 25 Ind Div, to express to 3 Co Bde the admiration we feel for their speed and fire in attack, and their aggressive and cheerful spirit when defensive actions have been imposed on them. 3 Cdo Bde has had a stern test – for many officers and men their baptism of fire – but they have emerged from it with a reputation of which all ranks must always be proud.[29]

The cost, however, had been extremely heavy, with 45 officers and ORs killed and a further 90 wounded.

Commandos take cover while launching a counterattack near Hill 170 as Japanese machine guns open fire, January 1945. (IND 4359)

Lessons learned

HMS *Princess Josephine Charlotte*. The raid on Dieppe was originally known as Operation *Rutter*, but was later renamed *Jubilee*. HMS *Princess Josephine Charlotte* XI was one of the landing ships tasked with transporting the assault infantry to Dieppe for the Operation *Rutter* raid, but was bombed by the Luftwaffe on the morning of 7 July 1942 while berthed in the Isle of Wight with the assault troops embarked. The damage caused to the vessel, together with the poor weather conditions, provoked the cancellation of *Rutter*. (A9756)

By the end of World War II, the Commandos – Army and Royal Marine – of the Special Service Group enjoyed a reputation amongst the British general public second to none, and had earned the admiration of most of their colleagues in the regular army and the healthy respect of their opponents. A stereotyped image of the Commando soldier, resplendent in distinctive green beret and insignia, as being a 'cutthroat, highly individualistic and with little regard to the niceties and discipline of ordinary military life' had become deeply entrenched in the popular mind as a result of skilful propaganda. Undoubtedly the Commando record was a proud one, with units deployed in Norway, France, Belgium, Holland, Germany, Africa, Egypt, Crete, Syria, the Adriatic coast and in the jungles of Arakan. A heavy butcher's bill had been paid, however, during the course of the war by these elite units. When No. 3 Commando landed in Normandy in 1944, for example, only two officers and a score of men still remained from those who had joined the unit in 1940, with the fighting at Vaagso, Agnone and Termoli having taken their toll. The number of gallantry awards to the Commandos speaks volumes about their achievements on various battlefields of World War II. A total of eight Victoria Crosses, 37 Distinguished Service Orders and a further nine bars to that award, 162 Military Crosses with 13 bars, 32 Distinguished Conduct Medals, and 218 Military Medals were awarded to Commando soldiers – a total that speaks for itself.

By war's end the Special Service Brigade had increased in size and its combat mission had evolved in a way never envisaged when it was first formed. Its ranks incorporated men of various nationalities united by wearing its distinctive Green Beret and Commando insignia. Although both worked well together in the field, relations between the Army and Royal Marines Commandos, however, remained strained. A deep-seated and enduring source of ill-feeling remained about the intrusion of another service into the Army Commandos' domain and whether 'pressed men' from Royal Marine units re-mustered into the Special Service Group in August 1943 were worthy of sharing the jealously guarded title 'Commando' and the Green Beret. Whether this criticism about the fighting quality of RM Commandos has any merit is a moot

HM King George VI awards a Military Medal to Cpl J.W. Hadfield, 41 (Royal Marine) Commando, at Creuilly, France, 16 July 1944. (B5624)

point. Perhaps controversially Robin Neillands, a historian of the Royal Marines, has written: 'Royal Marine units never, or at least rarely, achieved the same dash and flair as the best of the Army Commando units.' Similarly a former senior Commando officer concluded: 'I would have said that they were uneven. Some units were very good, some were, well – not so good.'

The Commandos' exact contribution to the British war effort in the final analysis was mixed and difficult to pin down. The early Commando raids from the UK were undoubtedly little more than pinpricks and until late 1942 the learning curve in terms of fighting methods and training for officers and men was undoubtedly steep. The history of the Middle East Commandos was one of missed opportunities and confusion, moreover, about the correct role and employment of these elite troops, who were largely wasted in a conventional role as a result of poor planning, limited resources and misapprehension about their capabilities. The volunteers stripped from regular units to man the Commandos undoubtedly lowered the efficiency of regular units, denying the rest of the British Army an opportunity to develop the offensive spirit. What is clear is that during the early war years the Commandos undoubtedly played a major and vital role in bolstering the morale of the British public and its armed forces in general by demonstrating a capacity to strike back offensively against the all-conquering German Wehrmacht. In the longer term, raids and threat of raids, moreover, successfully helped tie down large numbers of German troops in static, purely defensive duty, who otherwise might have played a critical role elsewhere.

The contribution made by the Commandos during the remainder of the war is more clear-cut. The Commandos – both Army and Royal Marine – clearly played an important part in final victory in North-West Europe and South-East Asia from 1943 onwards. Units of the Special Service Brigade/Group played a key and vital role in spearheading major amphibious operations and the ensuing pitched fighting, during which they fought alongside regular units. Following Madagascar and Dieppe, they increasingly became the 'steel tip' of the much larger amphibious shaft without which many opposed landings would have been far more difficult. In any event small-scale raiding was no longer their primary function post Dieppe with responsibility for small-scale raiding taken over by the Small Scale Raiding Force, No. 12 and 14 Commandos and the Special Boat Section.

The Commandos had also an indirect major effect on the course of World War II and upon the British Army as a whole in terms of lessons learned, despite the unfounded criticisms levelled against them by many senior regular officers, and the outright opposition to them from some quarters of the military hierarchy. The many and varied skills learnt and techniques developed by the Commandos had wider significance for the conduct of World War II and lasting importance to the present day. The innovative new equipment, fighting tactics and training methods developed by the Commandos and refined at Achnacarry were gradually adopted by the rest of the British Army, who tried in some respects to emulate the Commandos with the formation of 'Commando' or 'Guerrilla platoons' in some infantry battalions and 'Commando' training given at training establishments, in terms of physical fitness, weapon training and aggressive fighting methods. The experience and skills learnt during the execution and planning of small-scale Commando raids also entailed the development of new techniques, which in turn provided information needed to perfect methods later used for large-case combined operations, especially the June 1944 Normandy landings. Lastly, the example set and lessons learnt by the Commandos helped spawn various offshoots – including the Parachute Regiment, SAS, SBS, COPPs, the Beachhead Commandos, Special Operations Group and No. 30 Commando – which had an important impact on the conduct of World War II.

Ironically, the Army Commandos did not live on long after the end of hostilities, despite the contribution they had made to final Allied victory. On 25 October 1945 it was formally announced that the Army Commandos would be disbanded early the following year along with 'surplus' Royal Marine Commandos. Most former Commandos soon left the service or else returned to their original regiments where they often struggled to pass on their skills to the regular army. Many found their careers adversely affected by being former Commandos and failed to prosper. Henceforward the Royal Marines were made responsible for manning a single Commando Brigade, composed of three Royal Marine Commandos, for peacetime service, proudly retaining the distinctive title of Commando as part of their unit designations.

The Commando memorial, Spean Bridge
The Commando memorial was opened in 1952 at Spean Bridge in Invernessshire, Scotland to honour the memory of all those Commandos who died during World War II. Designed by Scott Sutherland of the Dundee College of Art, this imposing bronze sculpture of three Commandos, wearing battle dress, cap comforters and climbing boots looking out across the Great Glen, is a fitting tribute to the Special Service Brigade. An annual service of remembrance and wreath laying is held each November and attended by an ever-dwindling number of Commando veterans.

L Cpl Tickle, No. 48 (RM) Commando, and Marine Hardy, No. 46 (RM) Commando, being awarded military medals by General Bernard Montgomery, for bravery in Normandy. (B7391)

Chronology

1940	
May 1940	The Fall of France. Lochailort Special Training Centre opens to train Special Forces.
3 and 5 June	Churchill calls for a force to strike back against German-occupied Europe.
6 June	Idea of using a regular unit as basis for a raiding force abandoned.
9 June	War Office issues call for volunteers to Northern and Southern Command.
10 June	Lt Gen Sir John Dill appointed Chief of the Imperial General Staff.
June	Lt Col Dudley Clarke draws up Commando proposals for new CIGS. First Commando units formed.
12 June	General Sir Alan Bourne appointed as 'Commander, Offensive Operations'.
24/25 June	Operation *Collar* – raids by No. 11 Independent Company near Boulogne.
14/15 July	Operation *Ambassador* – raid by No. 3 Commando and No. 11 Independent Company on Guernsey.
17 July	Directorate of Combined Operations formed commanded by Adm Sir Roger Keyes.
July	MELF forms Middle East Commandos (Nos. 51 and 52).
August	No. 12 Commando formed in Northern Ireland.
November	Special Service Brigade formed by Brigadier Charles Haydon.
1941	
February/March	New Commando organization adopted.
February	Layforce despatched to the Middle East.
3 March	Operation *Claymore* – Lofoten Islands raid.
September	Lord Louis Mountbatten succeeds Keyes as ACO.
26–28 December	Operation *Anklet* – diversionary raid on Lofoten Islands.
27 December	Operation *Archery* – raid on South Vaagso.
1942	
February	Commando Depot opens at Achnacarry in Scotland.
February	A Commando Royal Marines formed at Deal, Kent.
27/28 March	Mountbatten promoted Vice Admiral and made Chief Combined Operations.
March	Operation *Chariot* – the St Nazaire raid.
June	No. 10 (Inter-Allied) Commando formed.
19 August	Operation *Jubilee* – the Dieppe raid.
30 September	Special Engineering Unit (later No. 30 Commando) formed.
7 October	B Commando, Royal Marines formed at Pembroke Dock.
18 October	Adolf Hitler issues his infamous 'Commando Order'.
11 November	No. 14 Commando formed.
November	A and B Commandos Royal Marine become 40 (RM) Command and 41 (RM) Commandos respectively.
November	Operation *Torch* – the invasion of North Africa.
1 December	Commando Mountain and Snow Warfare Camp opened at Braemar, Scotland.

1943	
12 April	A Special Service Brigade Advanced HQ formed at Prestwick. Operation *Husky* – the invasion of Sicily.
July	Special Service Group formed. Royal Marine Commandos join the Special Service Group and attend Achnacarry.
November	3rd Special Service Brigade departs for South-East Asia Command.
1944	
March	48 (RM) Commando formed as part of the Special Service Group.
6 June	The D-Day landings.
28 September	Third Arakan campaign begins.
1 November	Operation *Infatuate* – the capture of Walcheren Island.
6 December	Special Service designation changed to Commando.
1945	
31 January	Battle of Hill 170 in Arakan by 3rd Commando Brigade.
28 April	Third Arakan campaign ends.
1946	Disbandment of the Army Commandos.

Select bibliography

Combined Operations 1940–1942 (London: HMSO, 1943)
History of the Combined Operations Organization (London: 1956)
Rupert Butler, *Hand of Steel : the story of the Commandos* (Feltham: Hamlyn, 1980)
Stuart Chant-Sempill, *St Nazaire Commando* (London: Guild, 1985)
Mike Chappell, *Army Commandos 1940–45* (London: Osprey, 1996)
Thomas B.L. Churchill, *Commando Crusade* (London: William Kimber, 1987)
Ian Dear, *Ten Commando 1942–1945* (London: Leo Cooper, 1987)
Jon Cooksey, *Operation Chariot: the raid on St Nazaire* (London: Pen & Sword, 2005)
James Devins, *The Vaagso Raid* (London: Robert Hale, 1967)
James G. Dorrian, *Storming St Nazaire: the dock busting raid of 1942* (Barnesley: Leo Cooper, 2002)
Sally Dugan, *Commando. The elite fighting forces of the Second World War* (London: Channel 4 Books, 2001)
James Dunning, *The Fighting Fourth: No 4 Commando at war 1940–1945* (London: Sutton, 2003)
James Dunning, *"It Had to be Tough": the fascinating story of the origins of the Commandos and their special training in World War II* (Edinbugh: The Pentland Press, 2000)
Bernard Fergusson, *The Watery Maze: the story of Combined Operations* (London: Collins, 1961)
Ken Ford, *D-Day Commando: from Normandy to the Maas with 48 Royal Marine Commando* (London: Sutton, 2003)
Ken Ford, *St Nazaire 1942: the great Commando raid* (Oxford: Osprey, 2001)
Will Fowler, *The Commandos at Dieppe: rehearsal for D-Day* (London: Harper Collins, 2000)
Donald Gilchrest, *Castle Commando* (Edinburgh and London: Oliver and Boyd, 1960)
Cecil A. Hampshire, *The Beachhead Commandos* (London: Kimber, 1983)
W.G. Jenkins, *Commando Subaltern at War. Royal Marine operations in Yugoslavia and Italy 1944–1945* (London: Greenhill Books, 1996)
James Ladd, *Commandos and Rangers of World War II* (London: Macdonald and Janes, 1978)
Tony Mackenzie, 44 (R.M.) *Commando. Achnacarry to the Arakan: a diary of the Commando at war, August 1943 to March 1947* (Brighton: Tom Donovan, 1996)
Charles Messenger, *The Commandos 1940–46* (London: William Kimber, 1985)
Charles Messenger, *The Middle East Commandos* (London: William Kimber, 1988)
Derek Mills-Roberts, *Clash by Night: a Commando chronicle* (London: Kimber, 1956)
Raymond Mitchell, *Commando Despatch Rider: with 41 Royal Marines Commando in North-West Europe 1944–1945* (London: Leo Cooper, 2001)
Raymond Mitchell, *They Did What Was Asked of Them: 41 (Royal Marines) Commando 1942–1946* (Poole: Firebird, 1996)
J.L. Moulton, *Haste to the Battle: a Marine Commando at war* (London: Cassell, 1963)
Robin Neillands, *By Sea and Land: the Royal Marines Commandos – a history 1942–1982* (London: Weidenfeld & Nicholson, 1987)

Robin Neillands, *The Raiders. The Army Commandos 1940–46* (London, Weidenfeld and Nicholson, 1989)
Lucas Phillips, *The Greatest Raid of All* (London: William Heinemann, 1958)
Gerald Rawling, *Cinderella Operation: the battle for Walcheren, 1944* (London: Cassell, 1980)
Andrew Rawson, *Walcheren. Operation Infatuate* (London: Leo Cooper, 2003)
Hilary St George Saunders, *The Green Beret: the story of the Commandos 1940–1945* (London: Joseph, 1949)
Julian Thompson, *The Imperial War Museum Book of the War in Burma* (London, Sidgewick & Jackson, 2002)
Peter Young, *Commando* (London: Pan Ballantine, 1974)
Peter Young, *Storm from the Sea* (London: Wren Park, 2002)

Abbreviations

2i/c	Second in command
Adm	Admiral
ALC	Armoured landing craft
Brig	Brigadier
Capt	Captain
CBTC	Commando Basic Training Centre
Cdo	Commando
Cdr	Commander
Cdre	Commodore
CO	Commanding officer
COHQ	Combined Operations HQ
COPPs	Combined Operations Pilotage Parties
DCO	Director of Combined Operations
GOC	General officer commanding
HMS	His Majesty's Ship
IA	Inter-allied
LCA	Landing craft assault
LCT	Landing craft tank
LCI	Landing craft infantry
LMG	Light machine gun
Lt	Lieutenant
Lt Col	Lieutenant-Colonel
Lt Gen	Lieutenant-General
L/Corporal	Lance Corporal
LVT	Landing vehicle tracked
Maj	Major
ME	Middle East
MELF	Middle East Land Forces
MG	Machine gun
MGB	Motor gun boat
ML	Motor launch
MMG	Medium machine gun
MNBDO	Mobile Naval Base Defence Organization
MTB	Motor torpedo boat
NCO	Non-commissioned officer
OC	Officer commanding
ORs	Other ranks
RAMC	Royal Army Medical Corps
RAOC	Royal Army Ordnance Corps
RIN	Royal Indian Navy
RM	Royal Marine
RMBP	Royal Marine Boom Patrol
RN	Royal Navy
RQMS	Regimental Quartermaster Sergeant
RSM	Regimental Sergeant Major
RTU	Returned to Unit
SAS	Special Air Service
SBS	Special Boat Section
SIS	Special Intelligence Service
SOE	Special Operations Executive
SS	Special Service
SSRF	Small-Scale Raiding Force
UK	United Kingdom

Endnotes

1. Mike Chappell, *Army Commandos 1940–45*, (London, Osprey, 1996), p.4.
2. Cited in Charles Messenger, *The Commandos 1940–46*, (London: William Kimber, 1985), pp.25-6.
3. Ibid. pp.28-9.
4. Peter Young, *Commando* (London: Pan Ballantine, 1969), p.12.
5. Ibid, pp.158-9.
6. Messenger, op cit, pp.41-2.
7. Ibid, p.176.
8. Ibid, p.245.
9. Chappell, op cit, p.8.
10. Commando Training Instruction No. 1, 15th August 1940, National Archive WO 33/1668.
11. Chappell, op cit, p.9.
12. Stuart Chant-Sempill, *St Nazaire Commando* (London: Guild Publishing, 1985) p.7.
13. James Dunning, *"It Had to be Tough": the fascinating story of the origins of the Commandos and their special training in World War II* (Edinburgh: Pentland Press, 2000), p.72.
14. Tony Mackenzie, *44 (RM) Commando: Achnaccary to the Arakan. A Diary of the Commando at War, August 1943 to March 1947* (Brighton: Tom Donovan, 1996), p.77.
15. Thomas Churchill, *Commando Crusade* (London: William Kimber, 1987), p.67 and *Foreword* to Donald Gilchrist, *Castle Commando* (London: Oliver and Boyd, 1960).
16. Cited in Dunning , op cit, p.130.
17. SS Group Training Instruction No. 1. 24 October 1943, National Archive DEFE 2/1134.
18. Peter Young, op cit, p.34.
19. Messenger, op cit, p.34.
20. Brig. John Durnford-Slater, *Commando*, (London: William Kimber, 1953), p.22.
21. Ibid. p.70.
22. Young, op cit, p.58.
23. Ibid, p.56.
24. Maj. W.R. Sendall, 'The Royal Marine Landing at Westkapelle', National Archive, ADM 202/99.
25. Cited in Messenger, op cit, pp.300-301.
26. Messenger, op cit, p.394.
27. Young to Durnford-Slater, National Archive ADM 202/94.
28. Peter Young, *Storm from the Sea* (London: Wren Park, 2002), p.219.
29. 25th Indian Division Order of the Day by Major-General G.N. Wood, National Archive WO 203/4392.

Appendices

Appendix 1: outline history of Commando units, 1940–45

No. 1 Commando	No 1 Commando was raised during the late autumn of 1940 from existing Independent Companies. It carried out a series of small-scale cross-Channel raids and spearheaded the *Torch* landings in North Africa. It was then sent to the Far East as part of 3rd Special Service Brigade. It was later amalgamated with No. 5 Commando and was finally disbanded in 1946.
No. 2 Commando	No. 2 Commando was formed from volunteers selected across the UK and was intended from the outset to be a parachute unit. After it was reorganized as 11 Special Air Service Battalion (eventually renamed 1st Parachute Battalion) a new No. 2 Commando was formed. Following heavy casualties at St Nazaire, it reformed again and then served in the Mediterranean, carrying out operations in Sicily, Italy and Yugoslavia. It was disbanded in 1946.
No. 3 Commando	This unit was formed in July 1940 from volunteers, under the command of Lt Col John Durnford-Slater, and took part in one of the first Commando raids of World War II on the island of Guernsey. It took part in a large number of amphibious landings including the Lofoten Islands raid, Vaagso, and against the shore defences south of Dieppe in 1942. In 1943 it fought in Sicily and later Italy. After returning from the Mediterranean, it reorganized and joined 1st Special Service Brigade, commanded by Brig Lord Lovat, training for Operation *Overlord*. It landed on Sword Beach on 6 June 1944 and then relieved 6th Airborne Division at Pegasus Bridge near Caen. Following the defence of the Orne Bridgehead, No. 3 Commando was used in the final advance over the Rhine in 1945 and the pursuit to the River Elbe. It was disbanded in 1946.
No. 4 Commando	This unit was formed in March 1941 from volunteers from the British Army. It took part in various small-scale raids in 1941–42, including the raid on the Lofoten Islands in March 1941, Hardelot, and the Dieppe operations. As part of 4th Special Service Brigade it took part in the D-Day landings during which it captured Ouistreham and linked up with 6th Airborne Division. It then fought in the Orne Bridgehead where heavy casualties were suffered. In November 1944 No. 4 Commando took part in the Walcheren operations. It then rested and refitted and for the remainder of the war guarded the approaches to Antwerp. It was disbanded in 1946.
No. 5 Commando	No. 5 Commando was formed in mid 1940 from volunteers and during the early war years took part in various amphibious raids, including the landings on Madagascar. As part of 3rd Commando Brigade it was despatched to India in late 1943 and then fought in Arakan and Assam in 1944. Following the Third Arakan campaign in 1944–45, it underwent further intensive training for Operation *Zipper*. It amalgamated with No. 1 Commando and was finally disbanded in 1946.
No. 6 Commando	This Commando was raised from volunteers during the summer of 1940. In November 1942 No. 6 Commando took part in the *Torch* landings in North Africa and the ensuing fighting in Tunisia. It returned to the UK and landed in Normandy in June 1944. Following the breakout, No. 6 Commando took part in the crossings of the Juliana Canal, the River Rhine, River Weser, and the River Elbe. It was disbanded in 1946.
No. 7 Commando	This unit was formed in August 1940 in the UK. No. 7 Commando was then transferred to the Middle East as part of Layforce. It suffered heavy loses when it was committed to the defence of Crete, after which it was disbanded.

No. 8 Commando	This Commando was formed in the summer of 1940 from volunteers drawn primarily from the Brigade of Guards. It also fought in Crete, where acting as a rearguard it helped cover the final evacuation from the island. It was then disbanded after suffering heavy casualties.
No. 9 Commando	No. 9 Commando was raised from volunteers and men of the Independent Companies in mid 1940. Following operations based on Gibraltar, it served in the Italian campaign, in Greece and the Aegean. It was finally disbanded in 1946.
No. 10 (Inter-Allied) Commando	An initial attempt to raise No. 10 Commando from units in Northern Command in August 1940 met with little success, but early the following year a new No. 10 (Inter-Allied) Commando was formed. This unique unit eventually consisted of a Free French troop, a Dutch troop, a troop of men from Eastern European countries, a Norwegian troop, a Danish troop, a Polish troop, a Yugoslavia troop and later a further Free French troop. Its officers and men carried out a series of clandestine raids and operations behind enemy lines in Europe. Several fighting troops fought alongside men of other Commandos during the advance across North-West Europe, where their language skills and local knowledge proved of great value.
No. 11 (Scottish) Commando	No. 11 Commando was formed in mid 1940, under the command of Lt Col R. Pedder, from volunteers in Scottish Command. It became part of Layforce in early 1941 and garrisoned Cyprus for several months. It took part in operations on the Litani River in Syria in June 1941. In the late summer it was disbanded in Cyprus and its men dispersed to other units. It lived on briefly as No. 2 of the Middle East Commando and in November its men participated in the abortive attempt to kill or capture Rommel.
No. 12 Commando	This Commando was raised in Northern Ireland in early 1941 from volunteers. It took part in the diversionary raids on the Lofoten Islands (Operation *Anklet*) in December 1941. Although it participated in various small-scale operations, dwindling numbers meant this unit was finally disbanded in December 1943 and its remaining personnel were transferred to other units.
No. 14 Commando	This unit was raised in November 1942, commanded by Lt Col E.A. Wedderburn, specifically for special employment in extremely cold conditions in Norway following the long gap in operations in the region after the Vaagso raid. It consisted of two troops specializing in small boat operations and cross-country skiing respectively. After a string of abortive operations it was disbanded.
No. 30 Commando	This highly specialized unit was formed in 1941, alternatively known as 30th Assault Unit or the Special Engineering Unit, and consisted of No. 33 Royal Marine, No. 34 Army and No. 36 Royal Navy Sections, all of whom underwent Commando training. Its officers and men specialized in intelligence gathering, particularly in the immediate wake of major military operations and it was employed in North Africa, Sicily, Italy and North-West Europe. Detached sections followed closely behind leading units during the advance into Germany, for example, and secured vital intelligence from U-Boat bases.
No. 50 Commando	This was raised in 1940 from volunteers for Commando service in Egypt and Palestine and soon after formation amalgamated with No. 52 Commando to form D Battalion of Layforce. It was disbanded after the battle for Crete.
No. 51 Commando	This Commando was raised largely from Palestinian volunteers and fought in Abyssinia and Eritrea before being absorbed into the Middle East Commandos.
No. 52 Commando	No. 52 was also raised from volunteers from units in the Middle East before fighting in East Africa.
The Middle East Commando	The Middle East Commando was formed from the remnants of Layforce and assorted manpower from No. 51 and No. 52 Commandos to carry out raiding operations in the Middle East. It was disbanded in 1942.
No. 62 Commando	This unit formed in 1941 around a nucleus of existing Commandos operating under the auspices of the Special Operations Executive, and was known alternatively as the Small-Scale Raiding Force. Early in 1942 it 'cut out' three Axis ships from a Spanish port in West Africa and took part in various cross-Channel raids. Early in 1943 No. 62 Commando was disbanded with its personnel transferred to other units, including the SBS.

No. 40 (RM) Commando	The first Royal Marine Commando joined the Special Service Brigade in February 1942. Under the command of Lt Col Joseph Picton-Phillips, it was formed from volunteers from the Corps of Royal Marines and was known simply as A Commando, and its men attended the Commando Depot at Achnacarry. Following the disastrous Dieppe raid it was renamed No. 40 (Royal Marine) Commando. No. 40 (RM) Commando later took part in operations on the Adriatic coast. The disbandment of No. 40 (RM) Commando was completed on 21 January 1946.
No. 41 (RM) Commando	'B' (RM) Commando was raised at Pembroke Dock on 7 October 1942, commanded by Lt Col P.W. O'H. Phibbs, from men from 8th RM Battalion. It joined its sister Commando on the Isle of Wight where it was renamed No. 41 (RM) Commando. It fought in Sicily and at Salerno before returning to the UK in January 1944 in preparation for Operation *Overlord*. It fought as part of 4th Special Service during the D-Day landings and the ensuing fighting in the beachhead. It was withdrawn from the battle and after training took part in November in the Walcheren operations. For the remainder of the war it served on the Maas River front, before undertaking garrison duties in Germany. On 20 January 1946 it was disbanded.
No. 42 (RM) Commando	No. 42 (Royal Marine) was raised in August 1943, commanded by Lt Col R.C. de M. Leathes, from 1 RM Battalion as part of the expansion of the Commandos. As part of 3rd Special Service Brigade it served in India and Burma in 1943–45, including operations in Arakan and later Assam. It took part in the Third Arakan campaign where it carried out a series of amphibious operations down the lengthy coastline. It took part in the landings at Myebon before playing a major role in the fighting at Kangaw. It then returned to India Command to begin retraining for the invasion of Malaya.
No. 43 (RM) Commando	No. 43 (Royal Marine) was raised in August 1943, commanded by Lt Col R.W.B. Simons, from No. 2 RM Battalion as part of the expansion of the Commandos. It served as part of 2nd Special Service Brigade in Italy and the Adriatic coast before returning to Italy again where it fought until the general surrender of German forces in 1945. It had been disbanded by the end of January 1946.
No. 44 (RM) Commando	No. 44 Royal Marine Commando, commanded by Lt Col F.C. Horton, was raised in August 1943 with manpower drawn from 3rd RM Battalion (part of the disbanded Royal Marine Division). It passed through the Commando Depot at Achnacarry and was then posted to the Far East with 3rd Special Service Brigade. Following jungle training it briefly served in Arakan during the Japanese U-GO offensive, before carrying out several small-scale amphibious landings down the coast. During 1944–45 it served in the Third Arakan campaign and took part in a succession of amphibious landings along the coast, including the heavy fighting at Myebon and at Hill 170. It was then withdrawn to prepare for Operation *Zipper*.
No. 45 (RM) Commando	No. 45 (Royal Marine), commanded by Lt Col N.C. Ries, was raised in August 1943 from 5 RM Battalion as part of the expansion of the Commandos. Following a period of intensive training it joined 1st Special Service Brigade. On D-Day it landed on Sword Beach near Ouistreham and quickly pushed inland to relieve 6th Airborne Division. It took part in the ensuing fighting in the Orne Bridgehead and subsequent breakout before being withdrawn to the UK. In January 1945 it helped stem the German Ardennes offensive and then as part of 1st Commando Brigade took part in the advance into Germany. Following the end of the war, No. 45 (RM) Commando was despatched to the Far East to join 3rd Commando Brigade and remained as permanent unit.
No. 46 (RM) Commando	No. 46 (RM) Commando, commanded by Lt Col C.R. Hardy, was raised in August 1943 as part of the conversion of the Royal Marine Division into Commandos. It landed as part of 4th Special Service Brigade on D-Day and pushed inland in support of 6th Airborne Division and later served in the Orne Bridgehead. After suffering heavy casualties No. 46 (RM) Commando returned to the UK at the end of September to rest and refit. As part of 1st Commando Brigade it returned to the Continent in January 1945 where it guarded Antwerp from surprise attacks. No. 46 (RM) Commando participated in the advance into Germany during 1945, including several opposed river crossings, and briefly occupation duties. By the end of February 1946 it had been disbanded.
No. 47 (RM) Commando	No. 47 (Royal Marine), commanded by Lt Col C.F. Philips, was raised in August 1943 from

	10 RM Battalion as part of the conversion of the Royal Marine Division into Commandos. Following intensive training at Achnacarry, it became part of 4th Special Service Brigade. During the D-Day landings it helped capture Port-en-Bessin and served in the Orne Bridgehead and subsequent breakout. No. 47 (RM) Commando briefly retrained before taking part in the capture of Walcheren Island. It remained in the Maas River area until the end of the war. It disbanded on 31 January 1946.
No. 48 (RM) Commando	No. 48 (RM) Commando, commanded by Lt Col James Moulton, was the last Royal Marine Commando formed during the war and joined the order of battle of the Special Service Group in March 1944. It was formed from 7th RM Battalion and MNBDO II. It carried out a shortened course at the Commando Basic Training Centre before joining 4th Special Service Brigade in southern England. It took part in the D-Day landings in June 1944 and the ensuing fighting to protect the bridgehead in Normandy. It took part in the hard-fought Walcheren operations in November 1944. Following a brief rest it served in the River Maas area until the end of the war.

Appendix 2: Commando battle honours (arranged alphabetically)

Adriatic	Kangaw	Pursuit to Messina
Alethangyaw	Landing at Porto San Venere	Rhine
Aller	Landing in Sicily	St Nazaire
Anzio	Leese	Salerno
Argenta Gap	Litani	Sedjenane I
Burma 1944–45	Madagascar	Sicily 1943
Crete	Middle East 1941, 1942, 1944	Steamroller Farm
Dieppe	Monte Ornito	Syria 1941
Dives Crossing	Myebon	Termoli
Djebel Choucha	Normandy Landings	Vaagso
Flushing	North Africa 1941/43	Valli de Comacchio
Greece 1944–45	North-West Europe 1942, 1944, 1945	Westkapelle
Italy 1943–45	Norway 1941	

Index

References to illustrations are shown in **bold**.

aircraft 61, 63, 64, 72
Allen & Hanbury, Messrs, manager of 58
amphibious vehicles (LVTs), Buffalo and Weasel 72, **74**, 76
Arakan, battle for Hill 170: 77–79, **79**, **81**, 81–82, **82**
Arakan, South, amphibious landings **8**, **80**
Arethusa, HMS 63
Aschman, Seekommandant Kapitain zur See Frank 72
Australian Army 5

badge, Combined Operations **7**
Beatrix, HMS 16, 46, 55
Beattie, Lt Cdr Stephen 68
Belgian officers **11**
Boer Commandos 9
Boulogne area raids 13
Bourne, Gen Sir Alan 48, 49
British forces 85
  Armoured Division, 79th 74
  Canadian Division, 2nd 72
  Indian Corps, XV 77, 78
  Indian Division, 25th 78, 82
  Indian Infantry Brigade, 51st 79, 82
  Infantry Brigade, 155th 72, 74, 76
  KOSB, 4th & 5th 75
  Lancers, 19th 79
  Lowland Division, 52nd 72
  Royal Hussars, 13/18th **28**
Bruneval raid 49
Burma, central, amphibious landings **80**
Burroughs, R Adm H.M. 61

Calvert, Michael 36
Campbell-Hardy, Brig, DSO 77, 82
Campbeltown, HMS 67, 68, 70, 71
Caslon, Capt C. 54
casualties 32
Cator, Lt Col Henry 18
Chapman, Spencer 36
Chappell, Mike 4
Christison, Lt Gen Sir Philip 82
Churchill, Maj Jack **61**, 64
Churchill, Winston 4, 9, 11, 12, 13, 20, 53, 54
Clarke, Lt Col Dudley 9, 13, 50
combat mission 6–8
combat operations 53–55, 58–59, 61–68, 70–72, 74–79, 81–82
command 48–52
Commando Brigade, 1st (formerly 1st Special Service Brigade) **76**
Commando Brigade, 3rd (formerly 3rd Special Service Brigade) **8**
  Arakan, battle for Hill 170: 77–79, **79**, **81**, 81–82, **82**
  Arakan, order of battle, Jan–Feb 1945 **78**
Commando Depot (later Basic Training Centre), Achnacarry **21**, 21, 22, 31, **33**, 36–40, **39**, **40**, 41, **46**, 85
  order of battle, outline **37**
Commando Mountain and Snow Warfare Training Camp/Centre 40–41
communications 50, 51, 52
control 48–52
Copland, Maj Bill 14–15, 68
Courtney, Lt Roger 13

D-Day landings **5**, **43**, **44**
  see *also* Normandy landings; operations: *Overlord*
Daser, Generalleutnant Wilhelm 71
Dawson, Lt Col 72, 74
Dewing, Maj Gen R.H. 9–10
Dieppe raid 5, **6**, **8**, 22, 23, 25, **83**
doctrine 33–35
Durnford-Slater, Lt Col (later Brig) John **32**, 51, 54, 61, 64
Dutch officers **11**

equipment 45
Erebus, HMS 72
establishment, war, 24 February 1941 **17**
European recruits 22–23, 38, 39
  see *also* No. 10 (Inter-Allied) Commando

Fairbairn, Capt (later Maj) William 35, 36, 47
Fighting Troops 12, 16–17
Fohn 65, 66
Force Z 20
formation 9–13
  responsibility for **12**
  of Special Service Brigade 14–16
Fox-Davies, Lt Col 18
Franks, Maj G. **75**
French Commandos **11**, **21**, **33**, **34**

gallantry awards 82, 83
George VI. HM King **50**, **51**, **84**
German forces
  Division, 181st 59
  Infantry Division, 70th 71
  Infantry Division, 133rd 67
  Naval Artillery Battalion, 280th 66
  Naval Flak Brigade, 22nd 66
Glendinning, Col Will 50
Glenearn, HMS 16, 19–20
Glengyle, HMS 16, 19–20
Glenroy, HMS 16, 19–20
Graham, Lt Col J.M. 20
Guernsey operation 13, 53–54

Hadfield, Cpl J.W., MM **84**
Harrison, Lt Col S.S. 63
Haydon, Brig (later Brig Gen) Charles 14, 16, 37–38, 49, 50, 54, 61
Holland **29**, **30** see *also* Dutch officers; Walcheren assault
Hunt, Maj John 40–41
Hunton, Lt Gen T.L. **38**

Independent Companies 13
  No. 11: 13, 53–54
intelligence 49, 52
  see *also* No. 30 Commando
Irregular Warfare School, Inverailort Castle 36

Japanese Army, Imperial 77, 78, 82

Kangaw, Battle of see Arakan, battle for Hill 170
Kellerman, Harbour Commander 66
Kelly, HMS 49
Kenya, HMS 61, 63, 64
Keyes, Sir Roger 48–49
Killin, Perthshire **16**
Knowland, Lt George, VC 79
Krebs 55, 58

landing craft (LCI(S)) **44**, **52**
landing craft (MLC) **56**
Landing Craft, Armoured (ALC) **14**, 16, **30**, **62**, **63**, 64
Laycock, Maj Robert (later Maj Gen Sir Robert) 'Lucky' **6**, **11**, 19, 20, 25, 27, 29, 30, **48**, 50
Layforce 20
  Battalion, provisional order of battle, March 1941 **19**
  order of battle, March 1941 **19**
Leicester, Brig Bernard W. 'Jumbo' 71, **75**
Lister, Lt Col Dudley **11**, 22
Lofoten Islands raids 54–55, **55**, **56**, **57**, **58**, 58–59, **59**, 62, 63
Lovat, Lord **6**, 36

Madagascar raid 25
Mecke, Kapitain zur See Karl-Konrad 66
memorial, Spean Bridge **85**
Middle East Commando 18–21, 84
  provisional establishment, July 1940 **18**
Military Operations and Plans Directorate, MO9 section 9, 49, 50
Montgomery, Gen Bernard **32**, **85**
motor gun boat, MGB 314: 67, 68, 71
motor launches, Fairmile B 67, 68, 70, 71
motor torpedo boat, MTB 74: 67, 68, 71
Moulton, Lt Col (later Maj Gen) James L. 31, 74
Mountbatten, Cdre (later Vice Adm) Lord Louis **7**, 23, 24, 27, 38, 49–50, **59**, 65

NCOs, No. 48 (RM) Commando **29**, **53**
Neillands, Robin 84
Newman, Lt Col Charles 15, **66**, 67, 68, 70
No. 1 Commando 13, **14**, **24**, 25, 35, 41, 77, 78–79, 81
No. 2 Commando 13, 15, 32, 35, 45, 61, 62, 65
  St Nazaire raid 66–68, **69**, 70–71
No. 3 Commando 13, **16**, 16, 19–20, 25, 53, 54, 55, **57**, 83
  Vaagso raid 47, **59**, 61, 63–64, 65
No. 4 Commando **5**, 25, **28**, 41, **42**, 55, **57**
  Walcheren assault 71, 72, 74, 75, 76, 77

No. 5 Commando 25, 77, 79
No. 6 Commando 13, 25
No. 7 Commando 19–20
No. 8 Commando 13, 19–20
No. 10 (Inter-Allied) Commando **11**, 22–23, 41, 72, 75, 77
order of battle, 1944–45 **22**
No. 11 (Scottish) Commando 19–20, 45
No. 12 Commando 13, 15, 29, 41, 62
No. 14 Commando 24, 41
No. 30 Commando (Special Engineering Unit) 23
order of battle, 26 March 1943 **22**
No. 41 (Royal Marine) Commando 71, 72, 74, **75**, 75, 76, **84**
No. 42 (RM) Commando 31, 77, 78, 79, 81
No. 44 (RM) Commando 31, 77, 79
No. 46 (RM) Commando 31, **85**
No. 47 (RM) Commando 31, 71, 72, 75
No. 48 (RM) Commando **29**, 31, 41, **53**, 71, 72, 74–75
Y Troop **30**
No. 50/No. 51 Commando 18, 20
No. 52 Commando 18–19, 20
No. 62 Commando 23–24
Nonweiler, Brig W.I. 77
Normandy **28**
landings 47, **52**, 83, 85
see also D-Day landings; operations: *Overlord*
Norway 13, 24
Norwegian Army, Royal 61, 63
Norwegian officers **11**

officers **11**, **55**, **75**
Onslow, HMS 61, 65
Operational Holding Commando 40
order of battle, 1944 **37**
operations
Ambassador 13, 53–54
Anklet 62, 63
Archery **59**, 59, **60**, 61–66, **62**, **63**, **64**, **65**
see also Vaagso raid
ground component **61**
Avalanche 51
Bograt **30**
Chariot 66–68, **68**, **69**, 70–71
Claymore 54–55, **55**, **56**, **57**, **58**, 58–59, **59**
ground component **54**
Collar 13
Cordite 19–20
Husky 29, 51
Infatuate 71–72, **73**, **74**, 74–77, **75**
Jubilee **83** *see also* Dieppe raid
Overlord 30, 31, 41, **42**
see also D-Day landings; Normandy landings
Rutter *see* operations: *Jubilee*
Torch 23, 25, 29, 47, 50
orders of battle
June 1940 **10**
August/September 1943 **26**
organization 9–32
see also Special Service Brigade: formation of/growth of
early 9–13, **10**
expansion, April 1943 25, 27–32
Middle East, commandos in 18–21
reorganization, 1941 16–17
Oribi, HMS 61, 64, 65

Palmer, Lt Col E.C. 74
Phibbs, Lt Col O.H. 22
Phillips, Lt Col C.F. 75
Picton-Phillips, Lt Col Joseph 21
Polish officers **11**
Prince Albert, HMS 16
Prince Charles, HMS 61, 63, 64
Prince Leopold, HMS 61, 64
Princess Beatrix, HMS 16, 46, 55
Princess Josephine Charlotte, HMS **83**

Queen Emma, HMS 16, 46, 55, **58**

raids, cross-Channel, locations **7**
Rees-Jones, Geoffrey 41
Rhine crossing **76**
Rhodes raid 19–20
Roberts, HMS 72
Rommel, Gen Erwin, HQ raid 20
Royal Marine Commando 21–22, 83–84, 85
see also Nos. 42–48 (RM) Commando
Royal Marine Engineer Commando 31
order of battle, 1944 **27**
Royal Navy 61, 63–64, 65, 66, 67
Destroyer Flotilla, 6th 54, 55
Ryder, Cdr Robert, VC **67**, 67, 68

St Cecily raid **24**
St Nazaire raid 49, 66–68, **68**, **69**, 70–71
Saladin, HMS 53
Scimitar, HMS 53
ships, Dutch type landing 16, 17
ships, Glen-type assault 16, 17
Simpson, Col Adrian 18
ski training **16**
Small Scale Raiding Force 23–24
Smythe, Sqn Ldr Frank 40–41
Somali, HMS 55
Special Air Service Battalion, 11: 15
Special Boat Section 13
Special Service Battalions 14–16
No. 3 & No. 4: 54–55
composition, November 1940 **15**
order of battle, November 1940 **15**
Special Service Brigade(s) 4, 5, 32, 36, 40, 50, 83, 84
Advanced HQ 50, 51
order of battle **48**
changes to 25, 27–32
expansion 16–18
formation of 14–16
growth of 21–24
HQ 50
order of battle, March 1941 **18**
organization, March 1941 **17**
Rear HQ 51
order of battle **49**
Special Service Brigade, 1st (later 1st Commando Brigade) **42**, **43**
Special Service Brigade, 3rd (later 3rd Commando Brigade) 77
Special Service Brigade, 4th **44**, **52**
Walcheren assault 71, 72, 74
order of battle, November 1944 **72**
Special Service Group 30–31, 32, 41, 83, 84
HQ 51
order of battle, March 1944 **26**
Special Service Regiment, 1st 20
Sturgeon, HMS 67–68
Sturges, Maj Gen Robert 30
Sykes, Capt Eric 35, 36, 47

tactics 42–44
tanks, Sherman **28**, **78**
Tickle, L Cpl **85**
Tod, Maj Ronnie 13
Tovey, Adm Sir John 61, 63
training **14**, **21**, 21, **33**, 33–41, **40**, **46**
see also Commando Depot, Achnacarry
from late 1943 to the end of the war 41
ski **16**
Trevor, Lt Col Ken, DSO 78, 82
Tuna, HMS 61, 63
Tunisia 25, 51

uniform 45, 47, 83
US Army Rangers 5, **8**, 38–39

Vaagso raid **47**, 47, 49, **59**, 59, **60**, **61**, 61–66, **62**, **63**, **64**, **65**
Vaughan, Maj (later Col) Charles **21**, 37, **38**, 38
vehicles 17, 28

Walcheren assault 71–72, **73**, **74**, 74–77, **75**
War Office 10, 11, 18, 34
Warspite, HMS 72
weapons 45–47
anti-tank rifle, Boyes .55in. 13, 46, 47
carbine, De Lisle commando 47
grenades 46
knife, Fairbairn-Sykes fighting 35, 45, **47**, 47
knife and knuckleduster, Fanny combined 45
machine carbine, Sten 46
machine gun, Bren .303 light 12–13, 28, 45, 46
machine gun, Vickers .303 medium 28, 43–44, **45**, **46**, 47, **76**
machine gun, Vickers K light 47
mortar, 2in. 28, **47**
mortar, 2in. parachute 28, 46, **47**
mortar, 3in. 28, 32, 43–44, **47**, 47
PIAT (Projector Infantry Anti-Tank) 46, 47
pistol, US Colt .34in. 45
revolver, .38: 12, 45
rifle, Lee-Enfield .303 Short Magazine 12, 45–46
rifle, M1 Garand .30: 47
sub-machine gun, Thompson .45: 12–13, **34**, **45**, 45, 46
Wedderburn, Lt Col E.A.M. 24
Wills, Lt R.L. 59
Wood, Maj Gen N. 82

Young, Lt Col George 18
Young, Lt Col Peter 49, **51**, 78, 81